STITCH LOVE
Sweet Creatures Big & Small

Mollie Johanson

 LARK

For Nanny,

who let me stitch on her kitchen towels.

LARK

An Imprint of Sterling Publishing
387 Park Avenue South
New York, NY 10016

ISBN 978-1-4547-0809-4

Distributed in Canada by Sterling Publishing
c/o Canadian Manda Group, 664 Annette Street
Toronto, Ontario, Canada M6S 2C8
Distributed in the United Kingdom by GMC Distribution Services
Castle Place, 166 High Street, Lewes, East Sussex, England BN7 1XU
Distributed in Australia by Capricorn Link (Australia) Pty. Ltd.
P.O. Box 704, Windsor, NSW 2756, Australia

For information about custom editions, special sales, and premium and corporate purchases, please contact Sterling Special Sales at 800-805-5489 or specialsales@sterlingpublishing.com.

Email academic@larkbooks.com for information about desk and examination copies.
The complete policy can be found at larkcrafts.com.

Manufactured in China

2 4 6 8 10 9 7 5 3 1

larkcrafts.com

Contents

Introduction

If the Internet has taught us anything, it's that animals are cute. In fact, I'm not ashamed to say that while writing this book, I spent a fair amount of time looking up photos of cute animals. This is sometimes called "wasting time," but for me, it's "research." Researching cute animals is required for drawing cute animals, so I did what I had to do, and it paid off. Not only did I get a better idea for how these critters look, but I learned some fascinating things along the way—things that gave me a fresh perspective on the animals I was creating.

I already had a soft spot in my heart for sloths, but nothing prepared me for what would happen when I did a search for a video called "Bucket of Sloths." Try it. I'm sure you'll melt like I did! Then check out the result of my study in the embroidery on page 89. I even found myself looking through my grandpa's copy of the *Farmer's Almanac* and learning all about possums. They're not as bad as some people think they are, which is why the Precious Possum Hanging Sachet on page 55 is one of my favorite projects.

My experience is nothing new, however, because I've always loved cute things and learning more about them so that I can give them character and bring them to life with stitches through Wild Olive, my blog and pattern line (WildOlive.blogspot.com). And that's what this book is about: stitching cute critters to craft and love.

In the pages of this book you'll find plenty of creatures to choose from so you can create a sewn project or some simple embroidery, using craft methods that are as dear to me as the critters I've crafted. And there's practically a whole menagerie of motifs that you can stitch onto the projects or use on their own as you get creative.

Whether it's your beloved pet, the creature that you look forward to seeing at the zoo, or the sweet and silly bunny rabbit photo you found online (he's sticking his tongue out—how can you not fall in love with him?), everyone has an animal they adore. And if you're holding this book, I'm willing to bet that you also have a passion for creating.

Join me in combining these two loves by flipping through the pages and choosing your favorite stitched critter to make!

Awesome Outback Plush Trio

These animal friends each have their own house, which includes a clip so you can take them with you wherever you go!

Materials for the Animals

Embroidery Kit (page 106)

Templates (page 118)

Koala: Gray wool felt (about 6 x 8 inches [15.2 x 20.3 cm]) and small amounts of white and black wool felt

Kiwi: Dark brown wool felt (about 6 x 8 inches [15.2 x 20.3 cm]) and scraps of yellow wool felt

Kangaroo: Reddish brown wool felt (about 6 x 8 inches [15.2 x 20.3 cm]) and scraps of black wool felt

Embroidery floss, 1 skein each of colors to match the felt

Stuffing

Materials for the Carry Case

Sewing Kit (page 115)

Templates (page 120)

2 pieces of brightly colored cotton fabric, 4½ x 12 inches (11.4 x 30.5 cm) and 1½ x 3 inches (3.8 x 7.6 cm)

Gray wool felt, 4½ x 2¾ inches (11.4 x 7 cm)

Brightly colored wool felt, 2 x 3½ inches (5.1 x 8.9 cm)

Embroidery floss, 1 skein each of colors to match the fabric and felt

Key ring or carabiner clip

Note: makes one carry case

Stitches

Running stitch (page 116)

Backstitch (page 109)

Knot stitch (page 111)

Instructions

1 Using the templates and the photo as a color guide, cut out the pieces for each animal. You'll need two body pieces for the front and back, but all of the other pieces are a single layer.

2 Transfer and embroider the details onto each of the animal body front pieces using the tracing paper method, then appliqué the felt pieces in place using running stitch. Use three strands of embroidery floss throughout. A

3 Layer and pin the ears and limbs between the body pieces, then stitch around each animal with running stitch, leaving a small opening and making sure you catch the ears and limbs as you go. B

4 Fill each animal with just enough stuffing to make it soft and squishy. Stitch them closed with running stitch.

5 To make the carry case, press the small strip of cotton fabric in half lengthwise, then fold in the edges almost to the center and use running stitch along the open side to secure. This will be the side loop. C

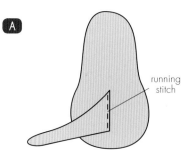

running stitch

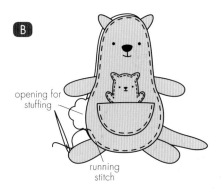

opening for stuffing

running stitch

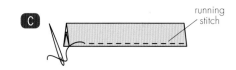

running stitch

6 Using tracing paper, embroider the rooflines onto the lower edge of the gray felt and the door details onto the colored felt. Use six strands of embroidery floss with backstitch for the lines and a knot stitch for the door handle.

7 Fold the big rectangle of fabric in half with wrong sides together, and pin the door to the top layer of fabric just above the crease. Stitch around the door using running stitch.

8 Press and pin the top edges of the fabric toward the wrong side to form a ⅜-inch (9.5 mm) hem, but don't sew it yet. Fold the side loop piece in half and place it on the left side of the case, ⅜ inch (9.5 mm) from the top edge, with the loop away from the edge.

9 Pin the right sides of the case together, then sew the two sides on a sewing machine with a ¼-inch (6 mm) seam, making sure the loop is securely attached. Turn the case right side out. **D**

10 Use running stitch along the front hem of the case. Place the plain side of the roof piece behind the case, then use running stitch to attach the roof and hem the back at the same time. **E**

11 Fold the roof down about 1¾ inches (4.4 cm), then use running stitch to create a ridge line ¼ inch (6 mm) from the fold. **F**

12 Add a key ring or carabiner clip to the loop. Repeat for the other two cases.

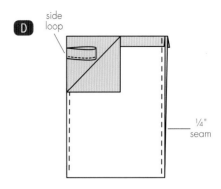

side loop

¼" seam

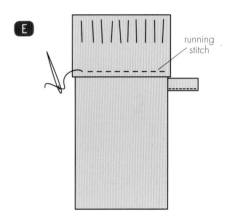

running stitch

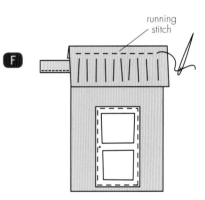

running stitch

Darling Dachshund Wrist Rest

This happy pup helps cushion your wrists while you're working at your computer keyboard. For extra comfort, pop him in a microwave and make him a hot dog!

Materials

Embroidery Kit (page 106)

Sewing Kit (page 113)

Templates (page 119)

Brown flannel, ¼ yard (22.9 cm)

Dark brown or black felt scraps

Embroidery floss, 1 skein of dark brown

Rice

Stitches

Running stitch (page 116)

Backstitch (page 109)

TRY THIS!

To warm your wrist rest, heat in a microwave for 90 seconds. You can also place it in a freezer for a chilly dog!

Instructions

Note: All seam allowances are ¼ inch (6 mm).

1 From the flannel, cut two bodies, two tails, four legs, and four ears.

2 Pin the pairs of tail, leg, and ear pieces right sides together. Sew around the edges, leaving an opening for turning.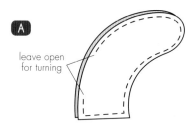

3 Turn the pieces right side out and sew the openings closed with ladder stitch (page 116). Stitch around each piece using running stitch and three strands of embroidery floss.

4 Cut two eyes and a nose from the felt. Appliqué the felt shapes to one end of a body piece and embroider the rest of the mouth using backstitch and six strands of embroidery floss.

5 Hand-sew the ears just above the face. Stitch the leg pieces to the second body piece, placing each leg about 4 inches (10.2 cm) in from the end.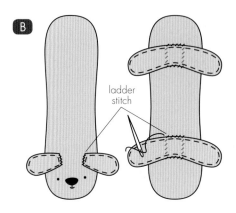

6 Pin the body pieces right sides together with the legs facing the front, but folded in so they are away from the edges. Place the tail between the layers at the back end.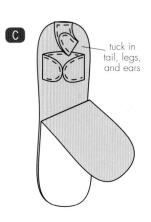

7 Sew around the body, leaving an opening at one end to turn. Turn the body right side out and topstitch around the body using running stitch, leaving the opening unstitched.

8 Fill the body with rice, then sew the opening closed with ladder stitch, and finish the topstitching.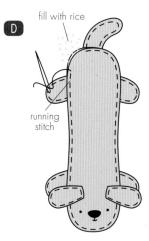

leave open for turning

ladder stitch

tuck in tail, legs, and ears

fill with rice

running stitch

Doodle Doo Apron

This friendly rooster may not actually wake you up in the morning, but he's sure to help with your breakfast preparations!

Materials

Embroidery Kit (page 106)

Sewing Kit (page 113)

Template (page 119)

Friendly Rooster and Footprint motifs (page 100)

Linen, 6 x 8 inches (15.2 x 20.3 cm)

Quilting cotton, 6 x 8 inches (15.2 x 20.3 cm)

Fusible interfacing, 6 x 8 inches (15.2 x 20.3 cm)

Kitchen towel or cloth napkin, approximately 18 x 18 inches (45.7 x 45.7 cm)

1-inch-wide (2.5 cm) twill tape, 2 yards (1.8 m)

Embroidery floss, 1 skein each of reddish brown, red, yellow, green, and black

Stitches

Running stitch (page 111)

Backstitch (page 109)

Knot stitch (page 111)

Stem stitch (page 112)

MORE ABOUT...
My grandpa raised chickens for many years, and believe me, most roosters aren't this friendly!

Instructions

Note: All seam allowances are ¼ inch (6 mm).

1 Trace the rooster motif onto the center of the linen. With six strands of embroidery floss, stitch the design using stem stitch for the tail and wing, knot stitches for the eyes, and backstitch for everything else.

2 Pin the quilting cotton onto the embroidered linen with right sides together. Sew straight across the top.

3 Flip the sewn fabric so that the wrong sides are together. Iron them together using fusible interfacing. Line up the top of the pocket template with the sewn edge, then pin and cut out the pocket. 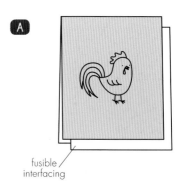 A

4 Sew the twill tape along the top edge of the front of the kitchen towel, making sure that the centers match up. Knot the ends of the tape.

5 Try on the apron to find where you want the pocket placed. Pin the pocket, then sew around the sides and bottom on a sewing machine. Add running stitch around the pocket for decoration, stitching through both the pocket and the apron along the bottom and sides but through the pocket only at the top edge. B

6 Use the tracing paper method to trace and then stitch some footprints along the top of the apron.

Tip: Cotton towels and napkins will shrink in the wash, so it's very important to launder your fabrics first!

A

fusible interfacing

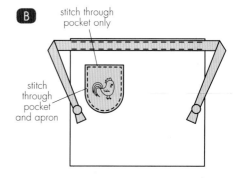

B

stitch through pocket only

stitch through pocket and apron

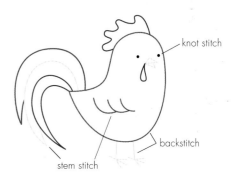

knot stitch

backstitch

stem stitch

backstitch

Festive Forest Friends
Felt Ornaments

These woodland critters are getting ready for the holidays and would love to adorn your tree!

Materials

Embroidery Kit (page 106)

Templates (page 120)

Chipmunk: Tan wool felt (about 4½ x 6½ inches [11.4 x 16.5 cm]) and small amounts of light brown, red, white, and green wool felt

Bird: Navy wool felt (about 8½ x 5½ inches [21.6 x 14 cm]) and small amounts of turquoise, red, green, and gray wool felt

Raccoon: Dark green wool felt (about 4½ x 6½ inches [11.4 x 16.5 cm]) and small amounts of gray, turquoise, and red wool felt

Embroidery floss, 1 skein each of black and colors to match your felt

Stuffing

Stitches

Appliqué stitch (page 115)

Backstitch (page 109)

Blanket stitch (page 115)

Knot stitch (page 111)

Satin stitch (page 112)

Straight stitch (page 112)

Lazy Daisy stitch (page 110)

Instructions

1 Using the templates, cut out all of the pieces for the ornament(s) you're making. Cut two backing pieces for each animal.

2 Before you start to stitch, lay out the pieces of the forest friends on their backing pieces to visualize how they will fit together, using the photo as a guide. Remove the top layers, leaving the bottom pieces.

3 Using three strands of embroidery floss that match the felt being used, sew the animal pieces onto each backing piece with appliqué stitch. Add the rest of the layers, stitching as you go. A

4 Transfer and then embroider the details on each ornament using the tracing paper method and three strands of floss.

5 Join the two backing pieces of each ornament using blanket stitch. Leave an opening, fill with stuffing, then close the opening using blanket stitch. B

6 Take a stitch through the top of the back of an ornament with six strands of floss. Bring the ends together and tie a knot about 2½ inches (6.4 cm) above the ornament to form a hanger. Repeat with each ornament. C

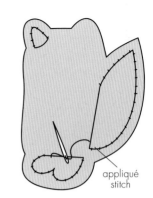

A

appliqué stitch

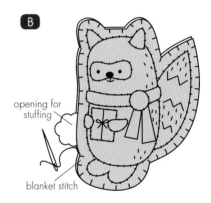

B

opening for stuffing

blanket stitch

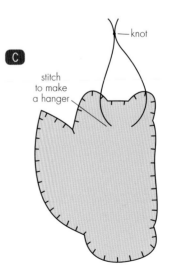

C

knot

stitch to make a hanger

Flighty Frog Pond Game

Help these frogs and lilies hop into their pond with this beanbag toss game!

Materials

Embroidery Kit (page 106)

Sewing Kit (page 113)

Templates (page 121)

Bright green fabric, ¼ yard (22.9 cm)

Blue fabric, ½ yard (45.7 cm)

Red fabric, small scraps

Yellow fabric, ¼ yard (22.9 cm)

Beans or rice

Perle cotton, 1 skein each of navy and bright green

Stitches

Backstitch (page 109)

Knot stitch (page 111)

Running stitch (page 111)

Instructions

Note: All seam allowances are ¼ inch (6 mm).

1 To make the game mat, cut two 16-inch (40.6 cm) squares from the blue fabric and cut three lily pads of different sizes from the green fabric.

2 Trace the embroidery designs onto the lily pads, then pin them onto one of the pieces of blue fabric. Use navy perle cotton to stitch the faces using backstitch and knot stitches.

3 Pin the right sides of the blue fabric together and sew around the edges, leaving an opening for turning. Clip the corners and turn the mat right side out. Hand-sew the opening closed with ladder stitch (page 116). **A**

4 Use bright green perle cotton and running stitch for the outlines and veins of the lily pads and to topstitch around the edges of the mat. **B**

5 To make the frogs, cut six bodies, six ¾ x 5-inch (1.9 x 12.7 cm) leg strips, and six ¾ x 2¾-inch (1.9 x 7 cm) arm strips from green fabric, and three tongues from red fabric.

6 Trace the eyes onto three frog bodies, then stitch using navy perle cotton and knot stitches.

7 Place two legs, two arms, and a tongue onto one body piece with right sides together, following the placement in the diagram. Baste in place. Repeat for each frog. **C**

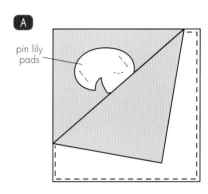

pin lily pads

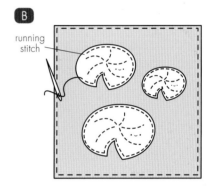

running stitch

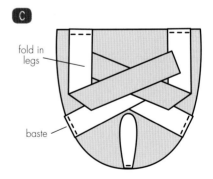

fold in legs

baste

8 Pin the plain body piece in place over the stitched body piece, taking care to tuck in the arms and legs so they won't get stitched into the edges. Sew around the frogs, leaving an opening for turning. Turn the frogs right side out.

9 Fill the frog beanbags with beans or rice, then hand-sew the openings closed with ladder stitch.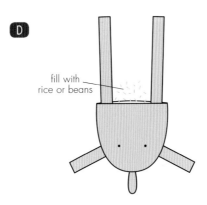

10 To make the lilies, cut six circles and 18 petals from yellow fabric using the templates.

11 Trace faces onto three circles, then use navy perle cotton to stitch the faces with backstitch and knot stitches.

12 Place six petals around the edge of the circles with faces, wrong side to right side. Baste in place. E

13 Pin the plain circles in place with right sides together. Sew around the lilies, leaving an opening for turning. Turn the lilies right side out.

14 Fill the lily beanbags with beans or rice, then hand-sew the openings closed with ladder stitch.

15 Reveal the faces on the lilies by opening up their petals!

D

fill with rice or beans

E

overlap petals

baste

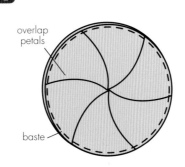

Fluttery Butterfly Pencil Topper

Slide this butterfly friend onto your favorite pencil, and she'll flit and flutter as you write!

Materials

Embroidery Kit (page 106)

Butterfly motif (below)

Linen, about 6 x 8 inches (15.2 x 20.3 cm)

Teal felt, 1½ x 1½ inches (3.8 x 3.8 cm)

Embroidery floss, 1 skein each of brown, orange, and black

Pencil

Stitches

Chain stitch (page 109)

Backstitch (page 109)

Running stitch (page 111)

Knot stitch (page 111)

Scallop stitch (page 110)

Tip: It's better if the felt body is just a little snug. You can easily stretch the felt out—it's harder to shrink it!

Instructions

1 Using the motif, trace and stitch two sets of wings onto the linen, spacing them at least 1 inch (2.5 cm) apart. Using three strands of embroidery floss, stitch the outlines in brown with chain stitch and the details in orange with backstitch.

2 Cut the wing sets apart, then pin them together with the wrong sides facing. Try to match up the stitching outlines as closely as you can. Using three strands of orange floss, stitch around the wing shape with running stitch. Cut around the shape loosely. **A**

3 Using black embroidery floss, embroider a face at the top center of the felt with knot stitches and a scallop stitch.

4 To create the body, wrap the felt firmly around a pencil, then carefully slide it off the end. Pin the felt to keep the shape, then use running stitch to secure the tube. **B**

5 Place the felt body on the center of the wings, then stitch the pieces together with two rows of running stitch. Work slowly and carefully to avoid sewing through the front of the butterfly body. **C**

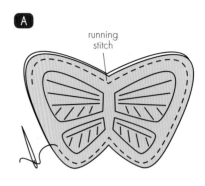

A running stitch

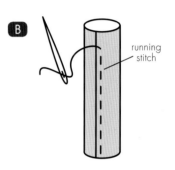

B running stitch

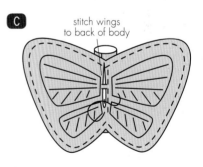

C stitch wings to back of body

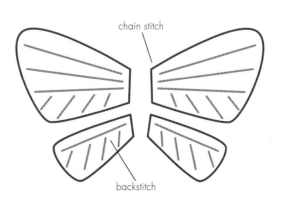

chain stitch

backstitch

Frozen Yeti Ice Pack

This frozen friend will keep you cool and get rid of those abominable boo-boos!

Materials

Embroidery Kit (page 106)

Templates (page 121)

White washcloth or small piece of white terry cloth

Light blue wool felt, 2 x 3 inches (5.1 x 7.6 cm)

Embroidery floss, 1 skein each of light blue, dark brown, and white

Pins

Stitches

Running stitch (page 111)
Blanket stitch (page 115)
Backstitch (page 109)
Knot stitch (page 111)
Satin Stitch (page 112)

TRY THIS!

This pouch is designed to hold ice cubes, but if you want to insert a reusable ice pack, resize the template to fit the pack you'll be using.

Instructions

1 Using the templates, cut out the yeti body and arm pieces from the washcloth and the face piece from the felt.

2 Embroider the details onto the body, arms, and face using six strands of embroidery floss and the tracing paper method. Attach the face to the body with running stitch and three strands of embroidery floss. A

3 Sew the bottom edge of the top back piece and the top edge of the bottom back piece with blanket stitch to help prevent fraying. B

4 Pin the arms in place, then pin the front and back pieces together with wrong sides facing. The back pieces will overlap in the middle. Sew around the outer edges using blanket stitch. C

Tip: Use caution when stitching through terry cloth, as the loops can pull. If they do, carefully trim the snagged pieces.

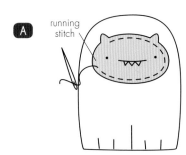

A — running stitch

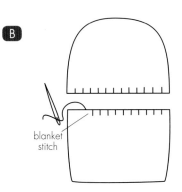

B — blanket stitch

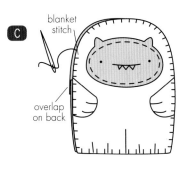

C — blanket stitch — overlap on back

Gleeful Guinea Pig Plush

This super-soft guinea pig loves getting snuggled so much that she sticks her tongue out with glee!

Materials

Embroidery Kit (page 106)

Sewing Kit (page 113)

Templates (page 122)

Brown anti-pill fleece, about
7 x 15 inches (17.8 x 38.1cm)

Cream anti-pill fleece, about
12 x 12 inches (30.5 x 30.5 cm)

Tan anti-pill fleece, about
12 x 12 inches (30.5 x 30.5 cm)

Pink wool felt, about
4 x 4 inches (10.2 x 10.2 cm)

Dark brown felt scraps

Light brown wool felt, about
2 x 3 inches (5.1 x 7.6 cm)

Stuffing

Brown thread

Embroidery floss, 1 skein each
of pink, dark brown, and white

Stitches

Appliqué stitch (page 115)

Knot stitch (page 111)

Running stitch (page 111)

Backstitch (page 109)

TRY THIS!
Prefer hamsters to guinea
pigs? Try shrinking this
down a bit for a smaller
critter friend!

Instructions

1 Using the templates, cut the body piece from brown fleece, then cut two 11-inch (27.9 cm) circles, one from cream fleece and one from tan fleece. A standard dinner plate makes an excellent template for the circles. Cut a nose, a tongue, and four feet from pink felt, two eyes from dark brown felt, and two ears from light brown felt.

2 Position the facial features on the center of the cream circle. Using appliqué stitch and three strands of matching floss, sew the eyes, nose, and top of the tongue in place. Fold the ears over by one-third and stitch along the straight edge with appliqué stitch, about 1 inch (2.5 cm) away from the eyes. A

3 Embroider the mouth with backstitch and add a white knot stitch on each eye for a highlight.

4 Sew a loose running stitch around the cream circle, then pull to gather, forming a pouch. Before tightening, fill the pouch with stuffing. Tighten the thread and secure it with a knot. Repeat with the tan circle. B

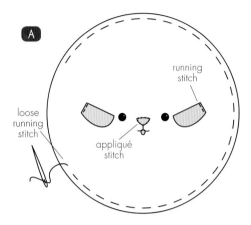

A

running stitch

loose running stitch

appliqué stitch

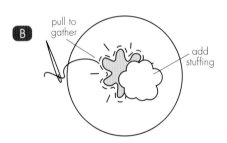

B

pull to gather

add stuffing

5 Wrap the body piece around the head, adjusting it so that the "fur" edges frame the face and the ends overlap at the bottom. Pin the body in place, then sew the edges to the head using appliqué stitch. Repeat on the other end.

6 Stuff the body section. Use enough to fill the body and make it taut, but avoid stuffing every crevice or it will look bulgy. Sew the bottom overlap closed. **C**

7 Stitch the four feet to the bottom. Use appliqué stitch along the back edges of the feet so that the toes remain free. **D**

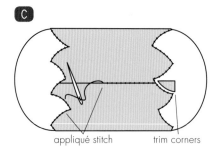

appliqué stitch   trim corners

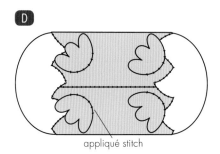

appliqué stitch

Tip: Where the fur corners overlap, you may need to trim the shaped edge so the fur matches.

MORE ABOUT . . .
When my mom was growing up, she had two guinea pigs named Ike and Mamie. They were like a married couple!

Glowing Fireflies Jar

Catching fireflies is a classic summertime activity. With this project you can keep your fiery friends all year round. They even glow in the dark!

Materials

Embroidery Kit (page 106)

Templates (page 122)

Red felt, about 3 x 3 inches
(7.6 x 7.6 cm)

Black felt, about 3 x 1½ inches
(7.6 x 3.8 cm)

Embroidery floss, 1 skein each of
black and glow-in-the-dark

Stuffing

Fabric, about 7 x 7 inches
(17.8 x 17.8 cm)

Glass jar with lid

Stitches

Straight stitch (page 112)

Knot stitch (page 111)

Scallop stitch (page 110)

Running stitch (page 116)

Backstitch (page 109)

TRY THIS!

Give your fireflies, or
"lightning bugs" as
they're sometimes called,
a more inviting home by
adding a felt leaf to the
jar. To make a firefly jar
that's more kid friendly,
use a plastic jar and
leave the fireflies loose
for easier play!

Instructions

1 Using the templates, cut six firefly bodies from red felt and three firefly wings from black felt.

2 Using the tracing paper method, embroider the faces and glow lines onto three of the body shapes. With three strands of black embroidery floss, make knot stitches for the eyes and tiny scallop stitches for the mouths. Use all the strands of glow-in-the-dark embroidery floss to make long, straight stitches for the glowing lines.

3 Stitch the wings onto the fireflies with a few straight stitches in the center.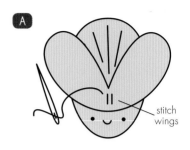

4 Sew a plain body piece to the bottom of each embroidered body piece using running stitch. Leave a tiny opening and fill each firefly with a small amount of stuffing. Stitch the opening closed. B

5 Using a bowl or plate as a template, cut a fabric circle a few inches larger in diameter than the lid of your jar. Holding the fabric over the lid, mark three spots where the fireflies will hang.

6 Tie a knot at one end of a single strand of black embroidery floss and take a stitch under the wings of a firefly, going from front to back so it will hang nicely. Stitch through one of the marked spots on the fabric and tie a knot so the firefly hangs at the level you want it to. Repeat with each firefly, varying the height at which they "fly." C

7 Hold the fabric over the opening of the jar, with the fireflies inside, then screw the lid in place.

A
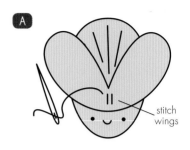
stitch
wings

B
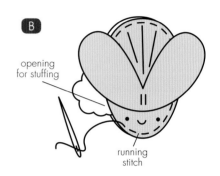
opening
for stuffing
running
stitch

C
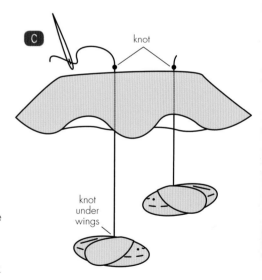
knot
knot
under
wings

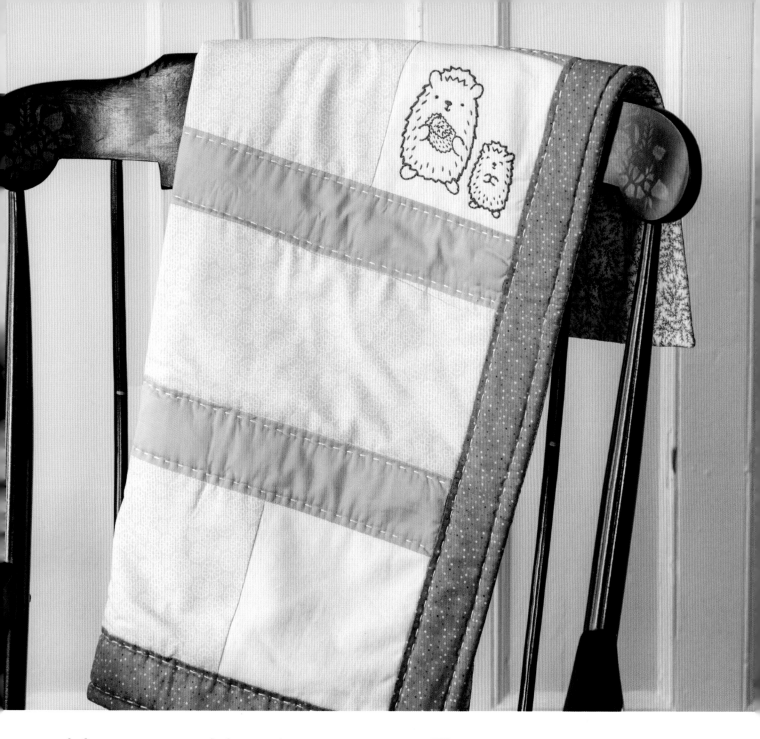

Happy Hedgehog Family Stroller Quilt

Even if you've never quilted before, you can make this simple mini-quilt featuring a family of hedgehogs and their new baby!

Finished size: 26 x 35 inches
(66 x 89 cm)

Materials

Embroidery Kit (page 106)

Sewing Kit (page 113)

Hedgehog Family motifs
(page 105)

Linen, ¼ yard (22.9 cm)

Yellow print fabric, ⅜ yard (34.3
cm)

Blue fabric, ¼ yard (22.9 cm)

Green print fabric, ⅜ yard (34.3
cm)

Backing fabric, ⅞ yard (80 cm)

Cotton batting, 27 x 36 inches
(68.6 x 91.4 cm)

Embroidery floss, 1 skein of brown

Perle cotton, 1 skein of cream

Stitches

Backstitch (page 109)

Scallop stitch (page 110)

Knot stitch (page 111)

Running stitch (page 116)

Straight stitch (page 112)

Satin stitch (page 112)

TRY THIS!

If hedgehogs aren't your
favorite, use another
animal family on your
quilt, or fill the squares
with lots of different
types of families!

Instructions

1 Cut the following pieces:

From the linen, cut four 6 x 6-inch
(15.2 x 15.2 cm) pieces.

From the yellow print fabric, cut four
6 x 16½-inch (15.2 x 41.9 cm)
pieces.

From the blue fabric, cut three 3 x
21¾-inch (7.6 x 55.2 cm) pieces.

From the green print fabric, cut two
3 x 27-inch (7.6 x 68.6 cm) pieces
and two 3 x 29½-inch (7.6 x 74.9
cm) pieces.

From the backing fabric, cut one 27
x 36-inch (68.6 x 91.4 cm) piece.

2 Assemble the quilt top using
¼-inch (6 mm) seams. Attach a
linen square to the short end of
each yellow rectangle, alternating
between the left and right ends.
Piece the blue strips between each
pieced strip. Sew the long green
edging strips along the sides and
then attach the remaining edging
strips to the top and bottom. A

3 Transfer the hedgehog family
motifs onto several of the linen
squares, then stitch the designs
with brown embroidery floss. Using

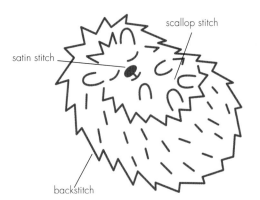

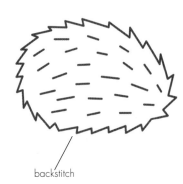

six strands and backstitch for the outlines, and three strands for the details: stitch the tiny curves with scallop stitch, the quills with small straight stitches, and the mama's eyes with knot stitches.

4 Cut the backing fabric and batting to match the quilt top. Use one layer of batting for a lightweight quilt or two layers for a heavier blanket.

5 Place the quilt with front and back right sides together, then pin them to the batting. Sew around the blanket, using ½-inch (1.3 cm) seams and leaving an opening for turning.

6 Clip the corners, turn the quilt right side out, then hand-stitch the opening closed using a ladder stitch (page 116).

7 Using perle cotton and running stitch, quilt along the top and bottom of the blue strips and around the inside and outside of the green borders.

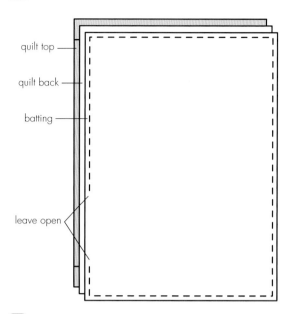

quilt top

quilt back

batting

leave open

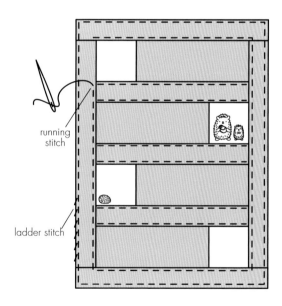

running stitch

ladder stitch

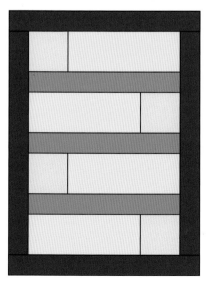

Holiday Mouse Furoshiki Cloth

This Japanese wrapping cloth is a fun and earth-friendly way to package gifts, especially with a mouse that's ready to celebrate!

Materials

Embroidery Kit (page 106)

Sewing Kit (page 113)

Holiday Mouse motif (page 97)

Linen or solid quilting cotton, 12 x 12 inches (30.5 x 30.5 cm)

Print fabric, 36 x 36 inches (91.4 x 91.4 cm)

Embroidery floss, 1 skein each of gray, pink, black, and colors for your chosen motif accessories

Stitches

Knot stitch (page 111)

Satin stitch (page 112)

Backstitch (page 109)

Lazy daisy (page 110)

TRY THIS!

Make different sizes and shapes for all kinds of gifts. Complete your crafted wrapping with a handmade tag safety-pinned onto the cloth.

Instructions

1 Choose a holiday mouse motif and transfer the pattern onto one corner of the plain fabric, then embroider the designs using three strands of embroidery floss for each color. Stitch the mouse body gray and use colors of your choosing for the accessories. Use knot stitches for the eyes, satin stitch for the nose, and backstitch for everything else.

2 Place the smaller fabric square on the corner of the larger fabric square with right sides together and with the embroidery toward the center. Sew a straight line across the smaller square, from corner to corner. A

3 Cut off the corner of the plain square, ¼ inch (6 mm) from the line of stitching. Press the embroidered corner down along the seam. B

4 Fold and press the hem over twice, and pin a hem along all four edges, then sew around the cloth. C

5 To use the cloth, place it on a table wrong side up with the gift in the center. Wrap the corner opposite the embroidery over the gift, then wrap the embroidered corner over the first fold. D E

6 Bring the remaining corners to the center and tie a knot. F

Tip: I made this cloth with the birthday mouse motif, but look on page 97 for other holiday options.

backstitch

lazy daisy

knot stitch

satin stitch

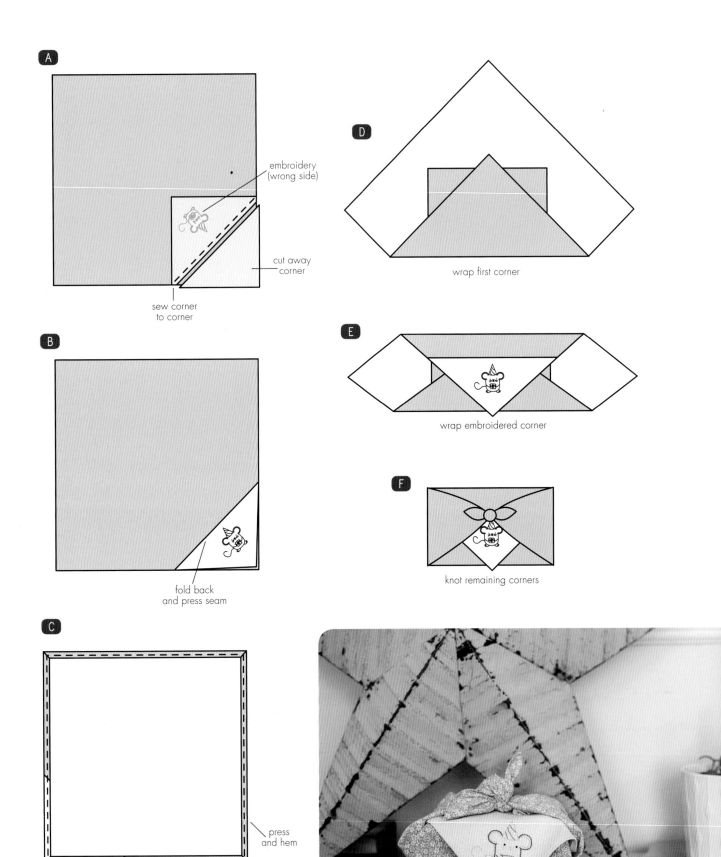

A

embroidery
(wrong side)

cut away
corner

sew corner
to corner

B

fold back
and press seam

C

press
and hem

D

wrap first corner

E

wrap embroidered corner

F

knot remaining corners

Hungry Critter Placemats

When it's mealtime, lay out these reversible placemats featuring woodland animals and the foods they like to munch!

Materials

Embroidery Kit (page 106)

Sewing Kit (page 113)

Hungry Critter and Food motifs (page 105)

Cream fabric, ⅓ yard (30.5 cm)

Print fabric, ¾ yard (68.6 cm)

Contrast fabric, ¾ yard (68.6 cm)

60-inch-wide (152.4 cm) thin cotton batting, ½ yard (45.7 cm)

Embroidery floss, 1 skein each of colors to match the motifs you choose

Note: Makes four placemats.

Stitches

Running stitch (page 111)

Knot stitch (page 111)

Satin stitch (page 112)

Stem stitch (page 112)

Straight stitch (page 112)

Cross-stitch (page 110)

TRY THIS!
Add extra critters to your placemats by stitching them on the reverse side as well.

Instructions

Note: All seam allowances are ¼ inch (6 mm).

1 Cut the following pieces:

From the cream fabric, cut four 5 x 12½-inch (12.7 x 31.8 cm) pieces.

From the print fabric, cut four 13 x 12½-inch (33 x 31.8 cm) pieces and four 5 x 12½-inch (12.7 x 31.8 cm) pieces.

From the contrast fabric, cut four 13 x 12½-inch (33 x 31.8 cm) pieces.

From the batting, cut four 17½ x 12½-inch (44.5 x 31.8 cm) pieces.

2 Choose two hungry critter embroidery motifs plus the foods that they enjoy eating. Transfer one design onto the bottom of each cream fabric strip. Using the photo and the motifs as a guide, embroider the designs with three strands of embroidery floss according to the patterns.

3 With right sides facing, sew an embroidered strip along the right edge of one of the large print pieces, and sew one 5-inch-wide (12.7 cm) print strip along the left edge of one of the contrast pieces. Press the seams toward the darker fabric. Ⓐ

4 Layer the placemat pieces together with right sides facing, and place these on top of one batting piece. Pin and then sew around the edges, leaving an opening to turn. Ⓑ

5 Clip the corners and turn the placemat right side out. Stitch the opening closed with ladder stitch (page 116).

6 Topstitch around the two sections of the placemats, using running stitch and three strands of embroidery floss. Repeat steps 3 through 6 to create the other three placemats. Ⓒ

MORE ABOUT . . .
Bears really do love honey, but they like eating the bees just as much.

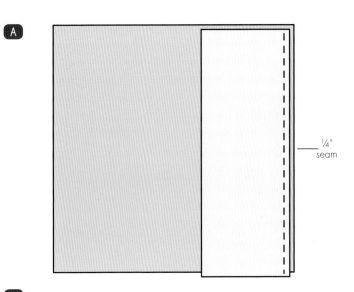

Ⓐ ¼" seam

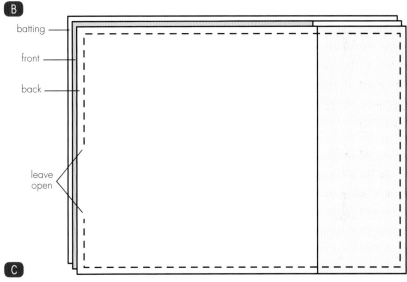

Ⓑ batting / front / back / leave open

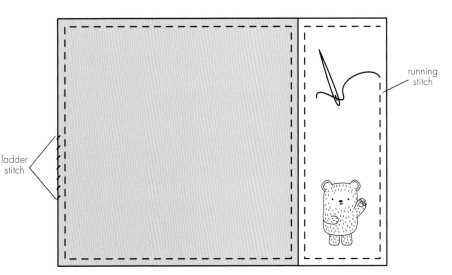

Ⓒ ladder stitch / running stitch

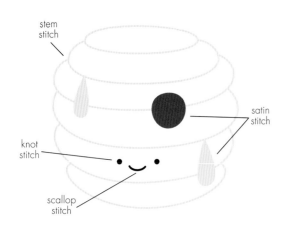

stem stitch

satin stitch

knot stitch

scallop stitch

stem stitch

knot stitch

scallop stitch

satin stitch

seed stitch

knot stitch

satin stitch

white

seed stitch

cross stitch

stem stitch

Inquisitive Owl Doorknob Hanger

Hang this sleepy-yet-curious owl on your doorknob and he'll always be ready
to ask "Hooooo's there?"

Materials

Embroidery Kit (page 108)

Sewing Kit (page 115)

Sleepy Owl motif (page 43)

Hooooo's There? motif (opposite)

Linen, one 5 x 6-inch (12.7 x 15.2 cm) piece and one 5 x 3-inch (12.7 x 7.6 cm) piece

Green fabric, one 5 x 12-inch (12.7 x 30.5 cm) piece and two 5 x 1½-inch (12.7 x 3.8 cm) pieces

Blue fabric, 5 x 1½ inches (12.7 x 3.8 cm)

Burgundy fabric, 5 x 1½ inches (12.7 x 3.8 cm)

Cotton batting, 5 x 12 inches (12.7 x 30.5 cm)

Ribbon, 10 inches (25.4 cm)

Embroidery floss, 1 skein each of brown, green, blue, yellow, and cream

Stitches

Backstitch (page 109)

Satin stitch (page 112)

Circle stitch (page 110)

Running stitch (page 111)

HOOOOO'S THERE?

backstitch

Instructions

Note: All seam allowances are ⅜ inch (9.5 mm).

1 Start by tracing and embroidering the motifs onto the linen pieces, with the owl on the larger piece. Using three strands of embroidery floss, stitch the outlines and letters with backstitch, the beak with satin stitch, and the sleep bubbles with circle stitch.

2 Sew a green strip to the bottom of the owl piece, followed by the blue strip, the burgundy strip, the second green strip, and finishing with the "Hooooo's There?" piece. Press all of the seams open.

3 Baste the ribbon hanger to the top of the owl section as shown in the diagram, then layer the green backing on top (face down) with the batting underneath. **A**

4 Pin and sew around the rectangle, leaving an opening for turning. Turn the doorknob hanger right side out and hand-sew the opening closed with ladder stitch (page 116).

5 Using three strands of cream embroidery floss, stitch around the outside edges and along the linen seams with running stitch. **B**

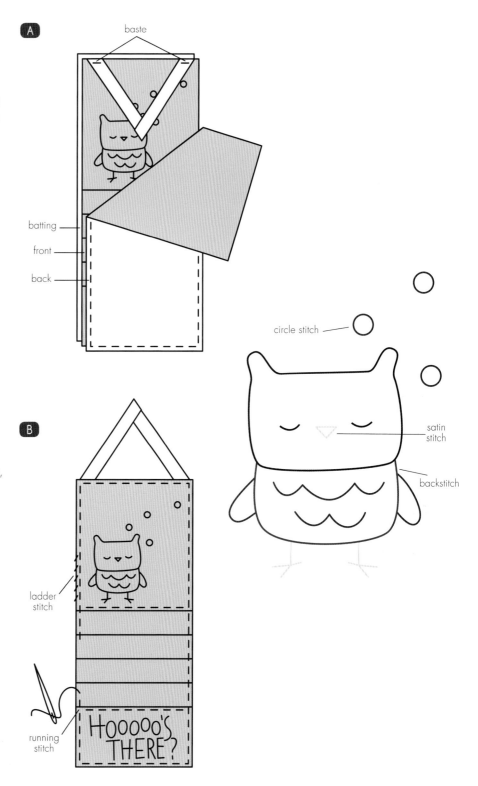

A

baste

batting

front

back

B

ladder stitch

running stitch

HOOOOO'S THERE?

circle stitch

satin stitch

backstitch

Lovely Ladybug Leaf Bag Tag

This lovely little ladybug will keep watch over your bag (and label it for you), all from the comfort of her leafy home!

Materials

Embroidery Kit (page 106)

Template (page 123)

Ladybug Leaf motif (page 100)

Green wool felt, two 5 x 7-inch (12.7 x 17.8 cm) pieces

Red fabric, 5 x 7 inches (12.7 x 17.8 cm)

Clear vinyl, 3 x 2¼ inches (7.6 x 5.7 cm)

Embroidery floss, 1 skein each of bright green, red, and black

¼-inch (6 mm) metal eyelet and setter

¼-inch-wide (6 mm) ribbon, about 12 inches (30.5 cm)

Heavy paper or cardstock, 3 x 2¼ inches (7.6 x 5.7 cm)

Stitches

Stem stitch (page 112)

Backstitch (page 109)

Knot stitch (page 111)

Running stitch (page 116)

TRY THIS!

Bag tags are perfect for luggage, diaper bags, gifts, or anything else that might need to be labeled! Switch out the ladybug for other leaf-loving critters.

Instructions

1 Transfer and embroider the ladybug leaf onto a piece of felt using the tracing paper method and six strands of embroidery floss. Use stem stitch for the leaf, and backstitch and knot stitches for the ladybug.

2 Use the template to cut out the felt leaf shape around the embroidery, along with a leaf from the red fabric. Cut the back leaf shape from the second piece of felt, including the opening and slit.

3 Stitch the vinyl behind the opening on the back leaf piece with running stitch and red floss. Use a sharp needle to pierce through the vinyl. A

4 Using running stitch and bright green floss, sew the three layers together so that the patterned side of the fabric shows through the window. **B**

5 Attach the eyelet at the right side of the leaf, following the manufacturer's instructions. Avoid cutting through the stitches. Thread the ribbon through the eyelet and tie the ends together. **C**

6 Write your name and contact information on the piece of paper and slide it into your bag tag.

A

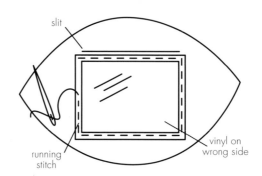

slit

running stitch

vinyl on wrong side

B

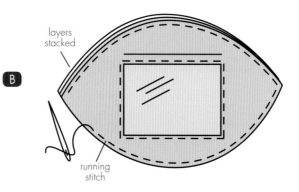

layers stacked

running stitch

C

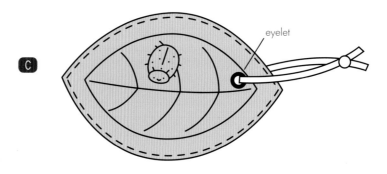

eyelet

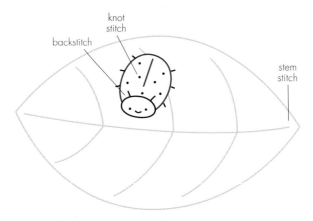

knot stitch

backstitch

stem stitch

Little Brown Bat Cap

Stitched onto brown felt, this sweet bat has the look of being filled in, without all the fill stitches!

Materials

Embroidery Kit (page 106)

Little Brown Bat motif (page 96)

Light brown wool felt, 4 x 5 inches (10.2 x 12.7 cm)

Embroidery floss, 1 skein each of brown, light brown, black, and white

Baseball cap

Stitches

Backstitch (page 109)

Knot stitch (page 111)

Satin stitch (page 112)

Straight stitch (page 112)

Running stitch (page 116)

Instructions

1 Use the tracing paper method to stitch the bat motif onto the felt. Using six strands of embroidery floss and the photo as a floss color guide, stitch the outlines, mouth, and teeth with backstitch, the eyes with knot stitches, the nose with satin stitch, and the wing details with straight stitch.

2 Cut around the embroidery, leaving about ⅛ inch (3 mm) of felt.

3 Pin the embroidered bat onto the front of the baseball cap at a slight angle. Sew around the edge with running stitch. A

TRY THIS!
Got a favorite team mascot? Use another animal motif to create a custom hat and show your team spirit.

A

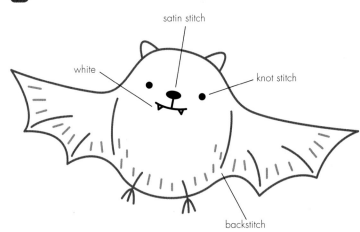

satin stitch

white

knot stitch

backstitch

running stitch

Pleasant Pet Shop Quiet Book

This soft book is a fun way for little ones to be quietly engaged as they look through the pages and "feed" the critters in the pet shop!

Materials

Embroidery Kit (page 106)

Sewing Kit (page 113)

Cat, Bunny, Mouse, Dog, Fish, and Parakeet motifs (page 98)

Pet Shop Window (page 123)

Templates (page 123)

Linen, seven 5½-inch (14 cm) squares

Quilting cotton, seven 5½-inch (14 cm) squares

Thin cotton batting, seven 5½-inch (14 cm) squares

Eight ⅜-inch (9.5 mm) metal eyelets (seven for the book, plus one for testing) and setter

Three pieces of ½-inch-wide (1.3 cm) twill tape, 18 inches (45.7 cm) long

Wool felt, small pieces of blue, orange, yellow, white, brown, and green

Embroidery floss, 1 skein each of teal, light teal, yellow, orange, gray, light brown, dark brown, yellow-green, pink, white, and black

Stitches

Stem stitch (page 112)

Knot stitch (page 111)

Satin stitch (page 112)

Backstitch (page 109)

Running stitch (page 116)

Instructions

1 Start by tracing the motifs onto the linen squares. Embroider the designs with three strands of embroidery floss, using stem stitch for the outlines, knot stitches for the eyes, satin stitch for the noses, and backstitch for the tiny details.

2 Layer the embroidered linen and quilting cotton squares, with right sides together, on the batting. Pin, then sew around all sides, leaving an opening to turn.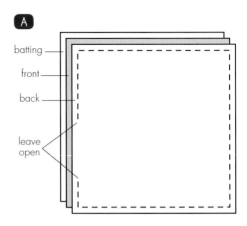

3 Clip the corners, then turn each page right side out and hand-sew the openings closed with ladder stitch (page 118).

4 Stitch around each page with running stitch.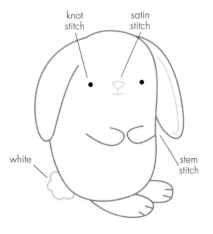

Tip: You may find it easier to stitch the designs on larger pieces of linen first, then cut them down to squares

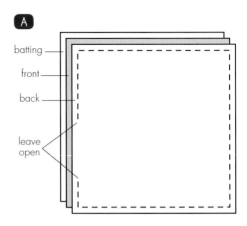

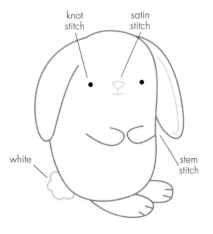

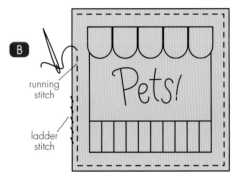

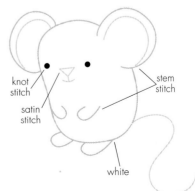

5 Install an eyelet in the top left corner of each page, following the manufacturer's instructions. It's a good idea to do a test eyelet first on layered scraps of fabrics and batting.

6 Stack the pages together, with the pet shop cover on top. Thread the three pieces of twill tape through the eyelets and, with all of the ends evenly aligned, tie a very tight knot close to the corner of the book. **C**

7 Using the templates, cut out two pieces of each of the foods from felt, and embroider details on one piece for the top.

8 At the end of each piece of twill tape, place two matching food pieces together and stitch around the edges with running stitch, making sure the tape is securely attached. **D**

Tip: Be sure to check the foods and eyelets on a regular basis so the book remains safe for young children.

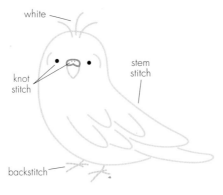

white

knot stitch

stem stitch

backstitch

MORE ABOUT . . .
Parakeets like fresh fruit and vegetables, so the parakeet in this book gets some yummy broccoli to munch on!

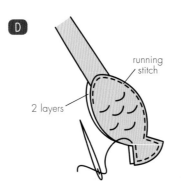

eyelet

tight knot

C

Pets!

satin stitch

knot stitch

backstitch

stem stitch

white

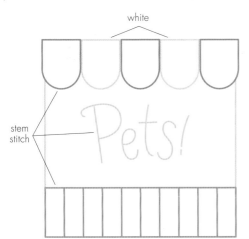

white

stem stitch

Pets!

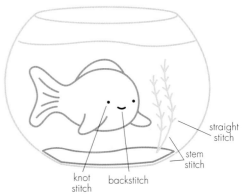

D

running stitch

2 layers

straight stitch

stem stitch

knot stitch

backstitch

Not-So-Terrifying T-Rex Pocket Pal Shirt

This dinosaur friend doesn't want to scare you . . . He just wants to add some whimsy to your wardrobe!

Materials

Embroidery Kit (page 106)

Not-So-Terrifying T-Rex motif (page 101)

Shirt with a pocket

Embroidery floss, 1 skein each of bright green, black, and white

Stitches

Knot stitch (page 111)

Backstitch (page 109)

TRY THIS!

Just about any critter would look sweet poking its head out of a pocket. And remember that pocket pals aren't limited to shirt pockets! Try adding them to tote bags or pockets on jeans.

Instructions

1 Begin by sizing the T-Rex to a proportion that looks best for the shirt pocket you are working with.

2 Transfer the motif onto the shirt so that it looks like it is coming out of the pocket. It's not necessary to transfer the entire design, but it should go down into the pocket at least ½ inch (1.3 cm). A

3 Embroider the T-Rex using six strands of embroidery floss for the outlines and three strands for the details. Use knot stitches for the eyes and backstitch for everything else.

A

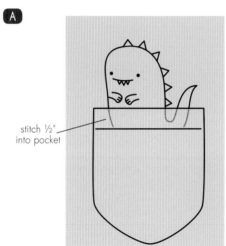

stitch ½" into pocket

knot stitch

white

backstitch

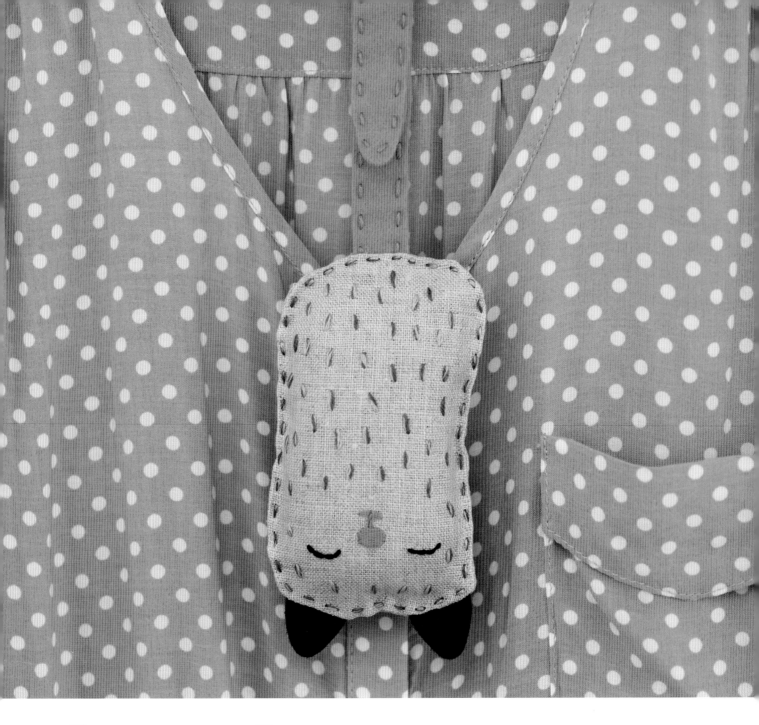

Precious Possum
Hanging Sachet

This sleepy possum just wants to hang out in your closet and keep your clothes smelling sweet!

Materials

Embroidery Kit (page 106)

Sewing Kit (page 113)

Templates (page 123)

Pink wool felt, 1½ x 9 inches (3.8 x 22.9 cm)

Small shank-style button

Linen, two 4 x 6-inch (10.2 x 15.2 cm) pieces

Black wool felt scraps

½ cup dried lavender or other scented filler

Poly pellets or other weighted filler (optional)

Embroidery floss, 1 skein each of dark gray, light gray, pink, and black

Stitches

Running stitch (page 116)

Backstitch (page 109)

Satin stitch (page 112)

Straight stitch (page 112)

MORE ABOUT . . .

Most people don't have a high regard for possums, but they're helpful for backyard ecosystems!

Instructions

1 Using the templates, cut two tail pieces from the pink felt. Cut a slit in one piece as shown on the template and sew the button on the curved end of the same piece. With the button on the outside, stitch the two tail pieces together with running stitch. **A**

2 Trace the possum pattern onto the linen, then embroider the design. Use satin stitch for the nose, backstitch for the eyes and mouth, and straight stitch for the fur. To give the fur a fun look, use three strands of dark gray embroidery floss and three strands of light gray mixed together as you stitch.

3 Cut out the embroidered possum piece, plus a second piece of plain linen for the back. Cut two ears from the black felt using the template.

4 Using the diagram as a guide, pin the ears and tail with the button side down on the embroidered possum and baste in place. **B**

5 Fold the tail up to the center, then pin the back in place. Sew around the body, leaving a gap for turning. Turn the possum right side out.

6 Fill the possum with lavender and some weighted filler so it hangs well. It should be full, but not tight. Hand-sew the opening closed with ladder stitch (page 116).

7 Stitch around the possum body with running stitch. **C**

8 To hang your sachet, loop the tail over a closet bar and tuck the button through the slit.

A

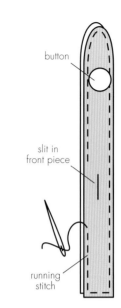

button

slit in front piece

running stitch

B

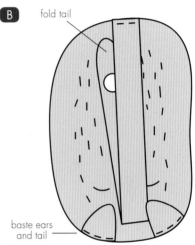

fold tail

baste ears and tail

C

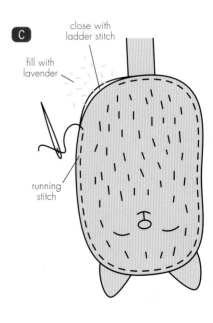

close with ladder stitch

fill with lavender

running stitch

Restless Robin
Drawstring Pouch

This robin is eager to go out hunting for breakfast, but she would gladly take the time to join you for an outing!

Materials

Embroidery Kit (page 106)

Sewing Kit (page 113)

Templates (page 124)

Heavy paper or cardstock

Linen, two 9 x 11-inch (22.9 x 27.9 cm) pieces

Red quilting cotton, two 9 x 11-inch (22.9 x 27.9 cm) pieces and one 6 x 6-inch (15.2 x 15.2 cm) piece

Brown quilting cotton, 6 x 6 inches (15.2 x 15.2 cm)

Yellow and dark brown felt scraps

Embroidery floss, 1 skein each of yellow and dark brown

Perle cotton, 1 skein of cream

1-inch-wide (2.5 cm) twill tape, 1 yard (0.9 m)

2 large wooden beads

Stitches

Running stitch (page 116)

Appliqué stitch (page 115)

TRY THIS!
Make this pouch in black and white, and you've got yourself a penguin pouch!

Instructions

1 Transfer the circle template to heavy paper. Pin the circle to the back of the small piece of red fabric. Cut around the circle, leaving a ⅜-inch (9.5 mm) margin of fabric.

2 Loosely stitch around the edge of fabric with running stitch, then pull it taut to gather the edge around the paper. Secure the thread with a knot, then press the edges and remove the paper.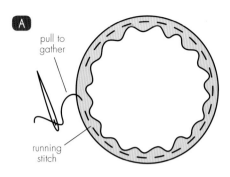

3 Use the templates to cut out a beak from yellow felt and two eyes from brown felt. Appliqué the pieces onto the circle (from step 2) to make the robin's face.

4 Cut out two pouch shapes from linen and two pouch shapes from red fabric. Hand-stitch the robin's face to a linen pouch piece toward the bottom, curved edge.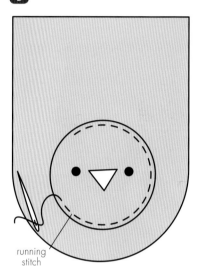

5 Make the wings by cutting four wing pieces (two regular and two reversed) from brown fabric. With right sides together, sew two edges together, leaving one open (as marked on the template). Turn the wings right side out.

6 With right sides facing, pin and sew each linen pouch piece to a red fabric pouch piece along the top, straight edge. Press the seams open. Pin the pouch pieces, right sides together, with linen to linen and red fabric to red fabric, matching the center seams as closely as you can. Pin the wings as shown between the linen layers. Sew around the pouch, leaving an opening in the side of the red fabric to turn.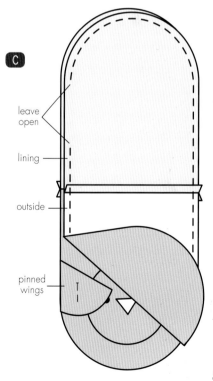

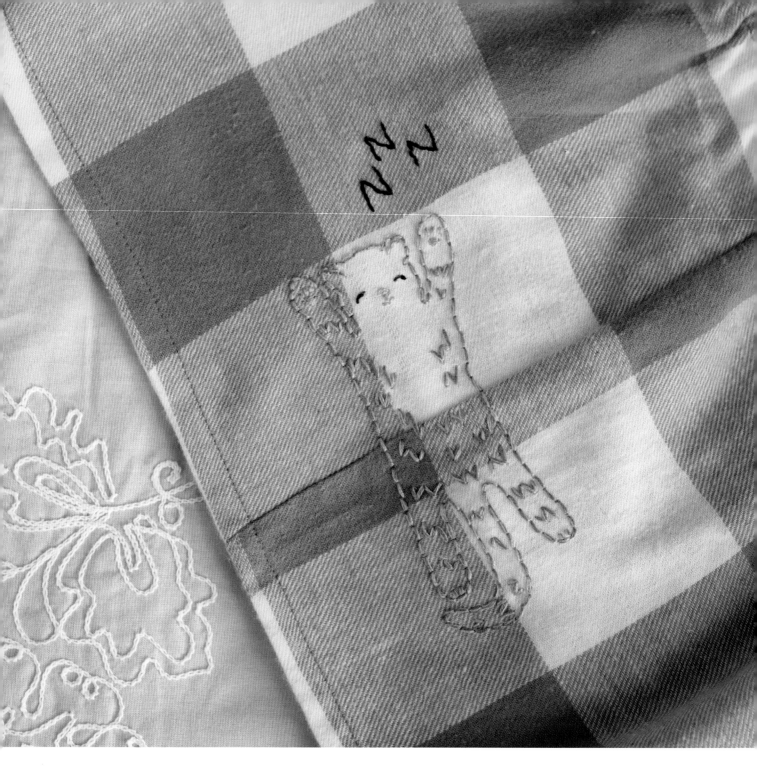

Sleepy Kitty Sleep Shorts

Feeling tired? It won't take long to stitch up a pair of sleep shorts featuring
a silly, stretching kitty.

Materials

Embroidery Kit (page 106)

Sleepy Kitty motif (page 99)

Ladies' sleep shorts or boxers

Embroidery floss, 1 skein each of yellow, orange, pink, and black

Stitches

Satin stitch (page 112)

Backstitch (page 109)

Scallop stitch (page 110)

Instructions

1 Begin by transferring the sleepy kitty motif onto the side of the shorts. If the shorts are flannel or any kind of thicker material, you may want to use the tracing paper method.

2 Embroider the design using six strands of embroidery floss for the outlines and fur and three strands for the details. Use satin stitch for the paws and nose, scallop stitch for the eyes and mouth, and backstitch for everything else. A

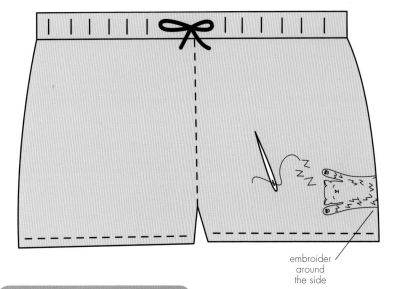

embroider around the side

TRY THIS!
To make the fur of your kitty look like a tabby cat, blend three strands each of yellow and orange embroidery floss.

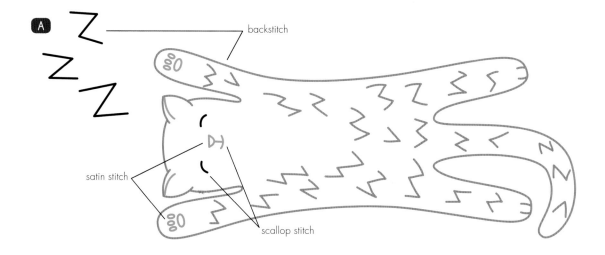

A

backstitch

satin stitch

scallop stitch

Sniffly Sea Turtle Tissue Cozy

This sweet sea turtle will keep tissues protected and easy to find for when you have a case of the sniffles!

Materials

Embroidery Kit (page 106)

Sewing Kit (page 113)

Templates (page 124)

Green felt, about 6 x 6 inches (15.2 x 15.2 cm)

Brown fabric, eight 1¾-inch (4.4 cm) square pieces

Tan fabric, seven 1¾-inch (4.4 cm) square pieces, two 2¼ x 6¼-inch (5.7 x 15.9 cm) pieces, and one 7¼ x 6¼-inch (18.4 x 15.9 cm) piece

Cotton batting, 7¼ x 6¼ inches (18.4 x 15.9 cm)

Embroidery floss, 1 skein of brown

Stitches

Running stitch (page 116)

Knot Stitch (page 111)

Scallop Stitch (page 110)

TRY THIS!
For a scrappier look, use little bits of stash fabrics in an assortment of bright colors.

Instructions

Note: All seam allowances are ¼ inch (6 mm).

1 Cut out the turtle's head, legs, and tail from the felt. You will need two heads and two tails and four pieces of each leg shape.

2 Embroider the face onto one of the head pieces, using knot stitch for the eyes and scallop stitch for the mouth, then stitch the head pieces together using running stitch around the edge. Do the same with the legs and tail, stitching the layers together. **A**

3 Sew the brown and tan squares together, alternating the colors in a checkerboard style and creating a grid with three rows of five squares. Press all of the seams open as you go.

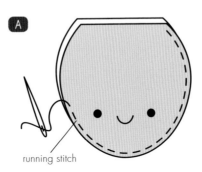

A

running stitch

4 Position the felt elements on the grid as shown, and baste in place. With right sides together, pin and sew the two small tan rectangles along the sides of the shell where the legs are. Press the seams toward the shell. **B**

5 Layer the larger piece of tan fabric on top of the turtle with right sides together, with the batting on the bottom of the stack. Pin and sew around the rectangle, leaving an opening to turn. **C**

6 Clip the corners, then turn the turtle right side out. Hand-sew the opening closed with ladder stitch.

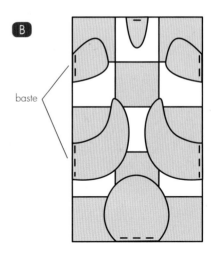

B

baste

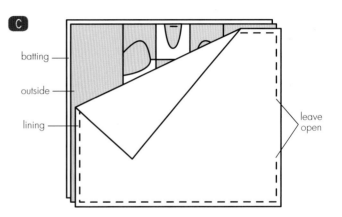

C

batting

outside

lining

leave open

7 Stitch a line of running stitch along the longer edge of the side panels and patchwork.

Tip: Stitching through all the layers can be hard on your fingers. A thimble will help!

8 Fold the side panels toward the back so they meet in the middle. Using a strong sewing needle and three strands of embroidery floss, stitch with running stitch along the head and tail ends to form the pouch. **D**

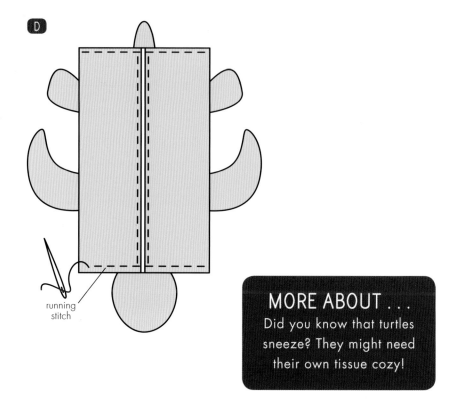

running stitch

MORE ABOUT . . .
Did you know that turtles sneeze? They might need their own tissue cozy!

Swift Snail's Trail Sweater

Fancy up a cardigan in no time with the addition of this not-so-slow snail!

Materials

Embroidery Kit (page 106)

Swift Snail motif (page 102)

Cardigan sweater

Two 5-inch (12.7 cm) squares of fabric, plus enough to cover all the buttons on the sweater

Fabric-covered button kit and as many button blanks as there are buttons on the sweater

Embroidery floss, 1 skein each of light brown, brown, orange, black, and a color to match your fabric

Stitches

Backstitch (page 109)

Knot stitch (page 111)

Scallop stitch (page 110)

Running stitch (page 116)

TRY THIS!
Snails come in all kinds of crazy colors, so don't be afraid to use bold shades!

Instructions

1 Trace the snail motif onto one piece of fabric, then stitch the design using six strands of embroidery floss for the outlines and three strands for the details. Use backstitch for the outlines, and knot stitches and a tiny scallop stitch for the face.

2 Cut around the embroidery, leaving a ⅜-inch (9.5 mm) border of fabric. Cut another piece of fabric to roughly match the embroidered piece.

3 Layer the two pieces of fabric and pin them onto the back of the cardigan near the bottom edge. Stitch around the snail with backstitch, using embroidery floss that matches your fabric, then add a running stitch trail behind the snail. Ⓐ

4 Cover the button blanks with the remaining fabric, following the manufacturer's instructions. Remove the sweater's original buttons and sew on the covered buttons in their place.

Tip: When sewing the snail's trail, take extra care. Stitching through finely knit sweaters can cause snags.

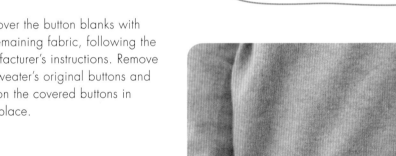

backstitch
scallop stitch
knot stitch

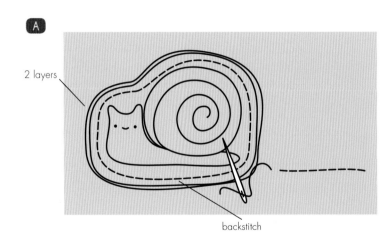

2 layers

backstitch

Undersea Buddies Brooch Trio

Group these three water-dwelling darlings together on a beach bag, or wear them separately on a trip to the aquarium!

Materials

Embroidery Kit (page 106)

Sea Creature motifs (page 104)

Linen, about 7 x 7 inches (17.8 x 17.8 cm)

Blue fabric, about 7 x 7 inches (17.8 x 17.8 cm)

Light gray felt, about 7 x 7 inches (17.8 x 17.8 cm)

Fusible interfacing, about 7 x 7 inches (17.8 x 17.8 cm)

Embroidery floss, 1 skein each of gray, teal, light blue, bright green, coral, cream, and black

Three sew-on pin backs

Iron

Note: Makes three brooches.

Stitches

Stem stitch (page 112)

Satin stitch (page 112)

Circle stitch (page 110)

Knot stitch (page 111)

Scallop stitch (page 110)

Backstitch (page 109)

Straight stitch (page 112)

Running stitch (page 116)

Instructions

1 Choose three sea creature motifs. Transfer the patterns onto the linen, then embroider the designs using three strands of embroidery floss. Use a combination of stitches for visual interest, using the motifs as a guide.

2 Iron the interfacing onto the back of the embroidery, being careful not to flatten the stitches.

3 Cut around the embroidered linen, leaving a ¼-inch (6 mm) border. Iron this onto the blue fabric, then cut around the shape, leaving a ⅛-inch (3 mm) border.

4 Lay the fused pieces onto the felt and cut around the shape, leaving a ⅛-inch (3 mm) border. Sew a pin back onto the back of the felt.

5 Lay the fused pieces onto the felt again and stitch around the edge of the linen with running stitch, using three strands of teal embroidery floss. A

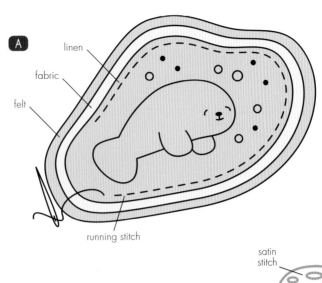

MORE ABOUT . . .
Although manatees move at a very slow pace, I could watch them for hours!

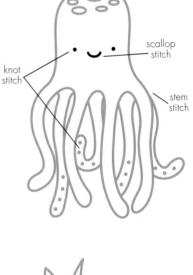

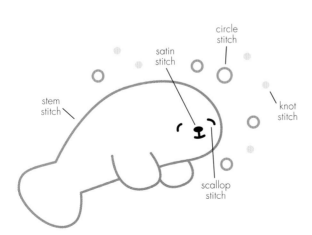

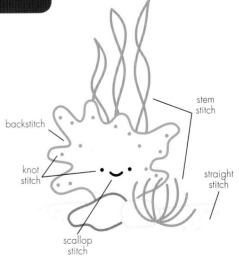

Whimsical Whale Wristlet

When you only need to keep a few necessities with you, this whale is here to help! His spray will hold him securely to your wrist.

Materials

Embroidery Kit (page 106)

Sewing Kit (page 113)

Template (page 124)

Gray corduroy, 9 x 13 inches (22.9 x 33 cm)

Blue print fabric, one 9 x 13-inch (22.9 x 33 cm) piece and one 1½ x 15-inch (3.8 x 38.1 cm) piece

Fusible interfacing, 9 x 13 inches (22.9 x 33 cm)

Embroidery floss, 1 skein each of black, gray, and blue to match the fabric

6-inch (15.2 cm) zipper, blue or gray

Small D-ring

Stitches

Knot stitch (page 111)

Backstitch (page 109)

Running stitch (page 111)

Instructions

1 Prepare the fabric by ironing the corduroy and large fabric piece together using fusible interfacing. Using the templates, cut out a front, a reversed back with zipper opening, and a flipper.

2 Embroider the face on the front, using the tracing paper method. Using six strands of black embroidery floss, make the eyes with knot stitch and the mouth with backstitch. Attach the flipper at an angle near the bottom using running stitch. A

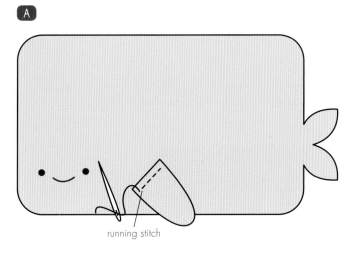

A

running stitch

3 Pin the zipper in the opening on the back piece, then sew around the zipper twice to make sure it stays secure. **B**

4 Cut a 2-inch (5.1 cm) piece off the end of the blue fabric strip. Fold and press each strip in half, wrong sides together, then sew along each strip, ¼ inch (6 mm) from the raw edge.

5 Fold the long strip in half and place the D-ring on the loop. Sew the ends of the loop together, back-stitching several times to keep the strap secure.

6 Fold the short strip over to create a loop, and thread it onto the D-ring. Place the short loop between the layers of the whale body (wrong sides together) above the face and pin the body pieces together. Sew around the main part of the body with a ¼-inch (6 mm) seam, avoiding the tail.

7 Stitch around the whale using three strands of blue embroidery floss and a running stitch. **C**

Tip: The raw edges of the strap will fray and become more charming over time. If you prefer to avoid fraying, use a product to seal the edge.

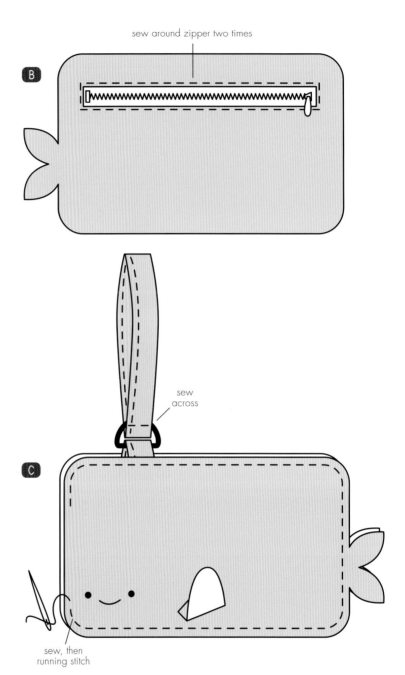

sew around zipper two times

B

sew across

C

sew, then running stitch

MORE ABOUT . . .
Whales can't breath through their mouths at all, which is why they have blowholes (er . . . wrist straps!).

Wild Animal Finger Puppets

Choose a favorite wild animal for your finger puppet, or make the whole set and act out a trip to the zoo!

Materials

Embroidery Kit (page 106)

Templates (page 125)

Lion: Yellow wool felt (about 3½ x 6 inches [8.9 x 15.2 cm]), reddish brown wool felt (about 2¾ x 2½ inches [7 x 6.4 cm])

Tiger: Orange wool felt (about 3½ x 6 inches [8.9 x 15.2 cm]) and scraps of dark brown wool felt

Elephant: Gray wool felt (about 4½ x 6 inches [11.4 x 15.2 cm])

Giraffe: Yellow wool felt (about 3½ x 6½ inches [8.9 x 16.5 cm]) and scraps of dark brown wool felt

Orangutan: Reddish brown wool felt, about 3½ x 6 inches (8.9 x 15.2 cm)

Embroidery floss, 1 skein each of black and colors to match the felt

Permanent fabric glue

Stitches

Knot stitch (page 111)

Satin stitch (page 112)

Backstitch (page 109)

Running stitch (page 116)

Instructions

1 Using the photo and templates as a guide, cut out the pieces for each finger puppet you are making. Cut two body pieces for each animal.

2 Layer and appliqué the head pieces and the body pieces: stitch the lion head to the mane, the tiger stripes to the front body, the elephant ears behind the head, the giraffe "horns" to the top of the head and the spots to the front body, and the orangutan muzzle to the lower half of the head. A

3 Using the tracing paper method, embroider the faces with three strands of black embroidery floss. Use knot stitches for the eyes, satin stitch for the lion and tiger nose, and backstitch for everything else.

4 Stitch the front and back body pieces together using a running stitch around the sides and top. B

5 Glue the head to the body using fabric glue, and allow to thoroughly dry. C

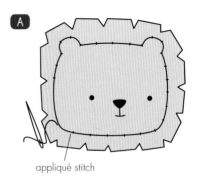

appliqué stitch

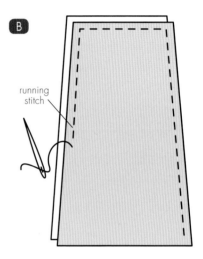

running stitch

glue

8

9

10

11

12

13

Farm

See page 100 for Friendly Rooster and Footprint motifs

Prairie

6

7

8

9

10

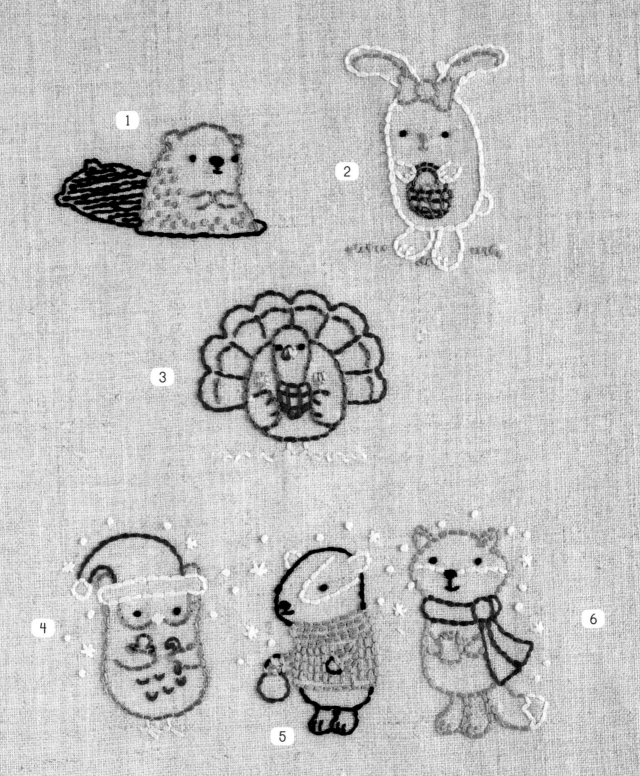

Holiday

Pets

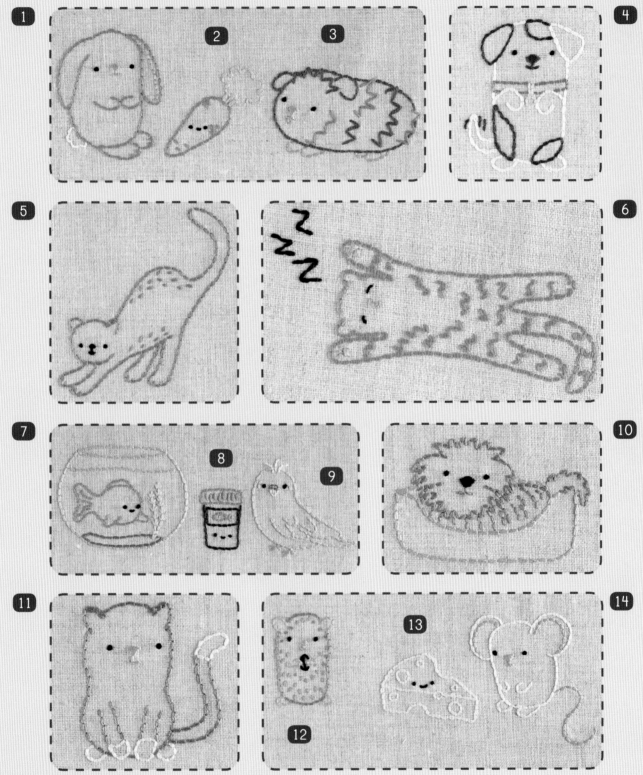

See page 98 for Pleasant Pet Shop Quiet Book motifs

7

8

9

10

11

Backyard

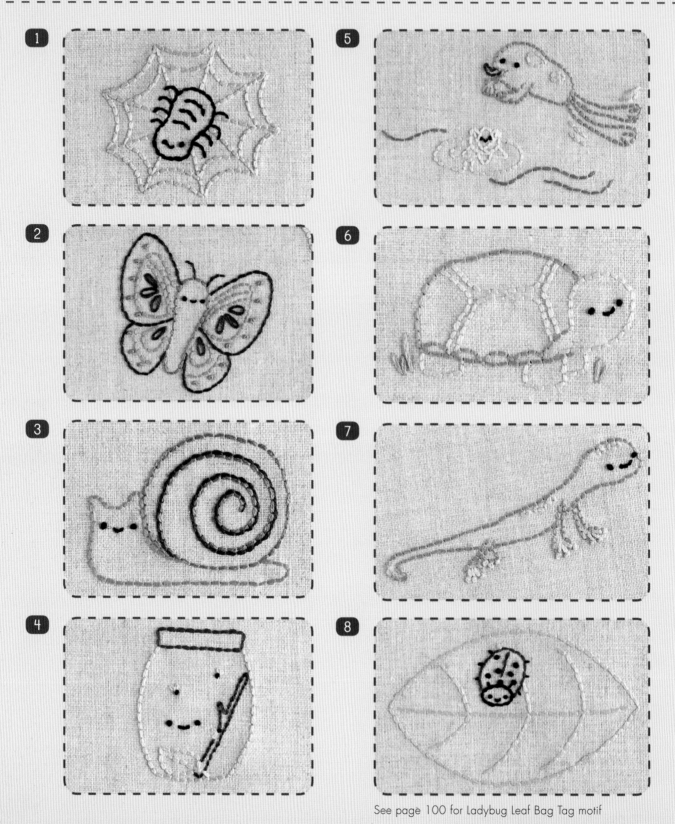

1

2

3

4

5

6

7

8

See page 100 for Ladybug Leaf Bag Tag motif

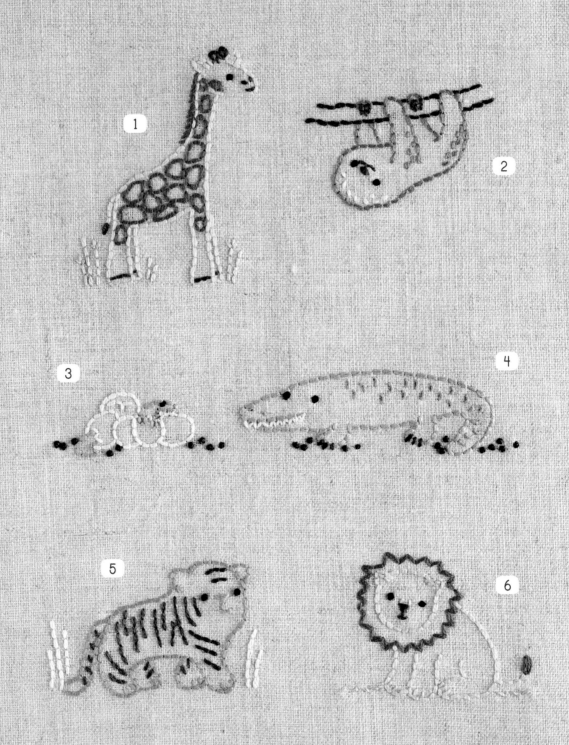

Wild

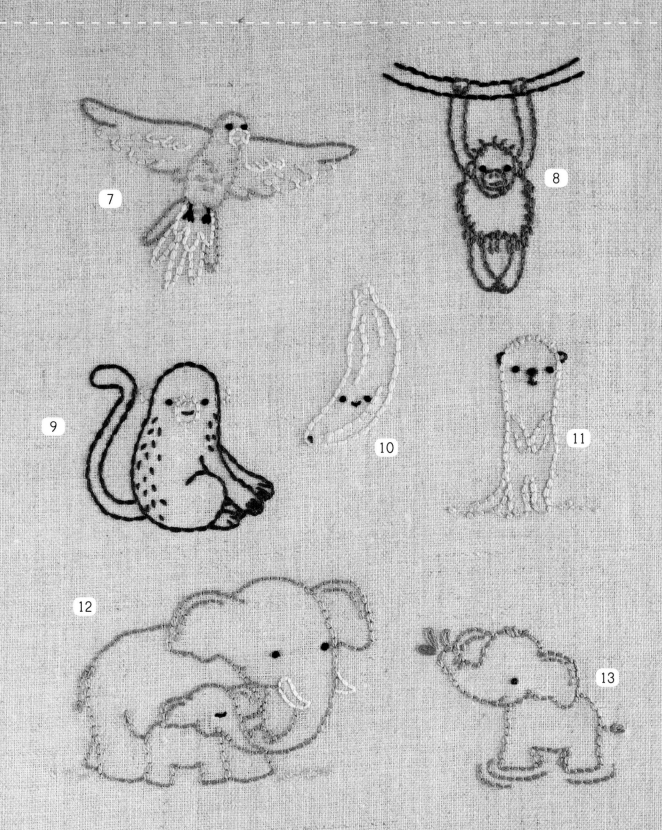

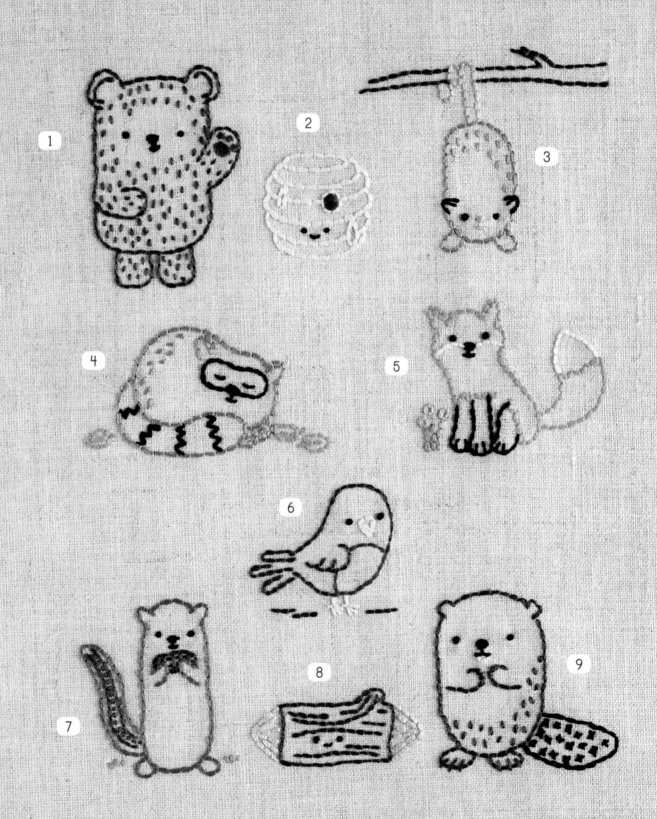

1

2

3

4

5

6

8

9

Layer these motifs to dress up your mouse! Simply skip the stitches that would be behind the overlapping pieces.

1

4

7

9

14

1

2

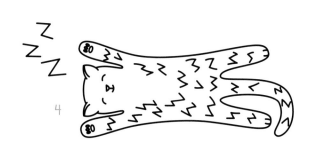

3

8

11

4

12

13

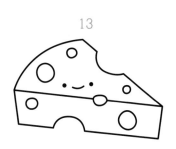

5

8

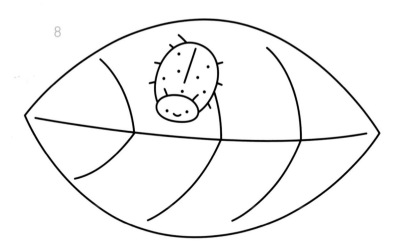

7

E mbroidery has been at the top of my list of favorite crafts for a long time. It's easy to learn, very portable, won't break the bank, and has endless possibilities. Embroidery often feels a bit like coloring in a picture with thread, which is quite relaxing. It's perfect for adding a sweet little animal to a blankie or shirt, or for creating the face on a plush pal.

You can stitch almost all of the motifs in this book with only two to three stitches (look for my Basic 3 on page 109), or you can expand and try out new stitches for a different look. You can use only the most basic supplies, or you can treat yourself to fancier tools and materials.

Embroidery Kit

When starting an embroidery project, you're going to need a few basic supplies on hand. The Embroidery Kit is used with every project in this book, and it's also what you'll need for stitching up any and all of the embroidery motifs!

EMBROIDERY KIT

Embroidery floss
Needles
Hoop
Scissors
Transfer tools & materials

Embroidery Floss:

One of the most basic supplies you'll use when stitching is embroidery floss. There are many varieties of floss available, so you have plenty of choices! For most embroidery, I prefer traditional cotton floss, which is made up of six strands and can be split to create different line thicknesses when stitching. Another option is perle cotton. This thread comes in different weights and is not designed to be split.

Be sure to use quality thread that is designed for embroidery, not just for crafts. It will cost a little more, but it holds up better, tangles less, and you'll be happier with the finished work. Each project has suggested colors, and the stitched motifs show examples to inspire you. Feel free to experiment with other color combinations and get creative!

TIP

As you stitch, your floss may untwist or become overly twisted. To fix this, simply let the needle and thread hang from your work until it spins itself to its natural state.

Needles:

You would think that a needle would be a simple tool, but there are actually lots of options. Don't get too overwhelmed though! Basically you need a needle that is large enough to fit three to six strands of floss through the eye. Needles labeled for embroidery or crewel will do nicely. Counted cross-stitch needles also work well, but they have a rounded point, making them less suitable when stitching through felt or using the tracing paper transfer method (see page 108).

Hoop:

Working with an embroidery hoop isn't absolutely necessary, and for some projects, it just doesn't work. However, most of the time, a hoop will make your stitching work much easier because it keeps the fabric (hopefully!) at an even tension. Whenever possible, choose a hoop that will accommodate the entire design you're stitching so that you don't flatten any stitches in the hoop. Most of the designs in this book will fit within a 6-inch (15.2 cm) hoop.

To hoop your fabric, loosen the screw on the outer ring and separate the pieces. Place the inner ring on a flat surface, lay your fabric over the hoop, and fit the outer ring onto the hoop. Tighten the screw to hold the tension.

Scissors:

When choosing scissors to use when stitching, I find the most important factor is that they cut well. That may sound silly since they're scissors, and of course you want them to cut well! The point here is that they should easily cut off a length of embroidery floss without chewing it and fraying the ends. Small embroidery scissors are handy because you can trim unused floss close to your work without cutting what you shouldn't.

Transfer Methods

Once you've chosen a motif to stitch, you need to get the design onto your fabric. There are lots of ways to do this, with different methods for different materials. You'll probably find that you end up with one or two that become your go-to transfer techniques!

Tracing

The simplest way to get your pattern onto whatever you're stitching is to trace it. A light box is a wonderful tool to have because you can start your project any time, but a sunny window does just as well. Copy your pattern onto regular white paper and tape it to your light box or window, then tape your fabric over the printed pattern so it won't shift while you're tracing.

To do the actual tracing, a water-soluble pen works great, and they come in different colors for working with different fabrics. Simply trace the lines with a light touch (so you don't get too much ink soaked into the fabric), embroider the design, then wash away the ink when you're done. You can also use a regular, well-sharpened pencil to trace the motifs onto most fabrics. The lines won't rinse away, but because they are very fine, your stitching will cover them.

Hot-Iron Transfer Pencil or Pen

Transfer pens and pencils work like traditional iron-on transfer patterns. You trace the motif onto regular or tracing paper, place the design face down on your fabric, then press the back with a hot iron, being careful not to shift the image. The design is reversed in the process, so you need to flip the image before tracing. These tools can be very handy, but the markings are permanent, so transfer carefully!

Tracing Paper

When working with dark fabrics like denim, or thick fabrics like felt, tracing paper is a great solution. To use this method, trace your chosen pattern onto tracing paper with a regular pen or pencil. Pin the paper onto your fabric, then stitch through the fabric and paper at the same time, following the lines on the tracing paper. When you've finished the design, carefully tear away the paper. Your stitches will have perforated the paper, making it easier to remove, but you still need to use care so you don't tug the stitches. In areas with tiny bits of paper left behind, use a needle or tweezers to remove the last scraps.

Water-Soluble Fabric or Paper

Like using tracing paper, this material is perfect for when it's difficult to trace a pattern onto your fabric. When working with water-soluble materials, you trace the motif(s) onto the stabilizer-like material, attach the material to your fabric (with pins, basting, or adhesive) and stitch through the fabric and pattern. When you're finished with the embroidery, you simply soak the fabric, and the water-soluble material magically washes away. With some kinds of water-soluble fabric, you can even print onto them with an ink-jet printer to make it even easier!

STARTING & STOPPING

Before you start stitching, you need to choose whether to knot . . . or not. Many people tell you to start without a knot, securing the end of the thread on the back by going over it with your first four or five stitches. While I've used the knotless method for a long time, starting with a knot is easier and more secure, especially if your stitching will get washed.

To keep the back of your work tidy, combine the two methods! Tie a knot, but leave a tail that's about 1 inch (2.5 cm) long. When you start your embroidery, stitch over the tail to hold it in place.

Similarly, when you finish stitching an area, tie a knot close to the fabric on the back of your work, then use your needle to weave the floss through the back of a few stitches before trimming the thread.

Embroidery Stitches

Although you could spend years learning every embroidery stitch there ever was, for most stitching projects you can work from a small selection of stitches. You'll find diagrams with suggested stitches throughout the projects, but there's really no right or wrong way to put these stitches to use. Mix them up—your embroidery will come to life!

BASIC 3

If you're new to embroidery, or are simply looking for the quickest way to get stitching, these are the stitches I recommend that you start out with. They're the basics you'll want for outlining and stitching eyes and faces.

- Backstitch
- Knot Stitch
- Scallop Stitch

Backstitch

Backstitch is my favorite way to outline a design. It's easy to learn and has a cute, casual look!

Bring the needle up at point 1 and go down at point 2, then come up at point 3, and down at point 4. Repeat this process, following the motif lines.

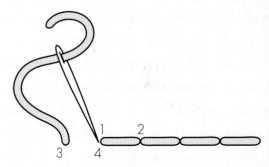

Chain Stitch

Chain stitch creates a line of linked stitches that really do look like a little chain. I like using this stitch when I want to make an outline with some texture. There are two ways to work the stitch: forward (classic!) and reverse (easy peasy!).

To **forward chain stitch**, bring the needle up at point 1 and down at point 1, eaving a small loop of thread. Come up through the loop at point 2 and down at point 2, leaving a small loop. Repeat this process, then when you're at the end of your line of stitching, tack down the last loop with a small stitch.

To **reverse chain stitch**, make a small straight stitch along your stitching line. Bring the needle up at point 1, slide the needle under the small straight stitch, then go down at point 1. Come up at point 2, slide the needle under the previous stitch, then go back down at point 2. Repeat this process.

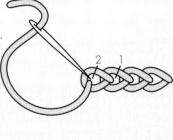

Circle Stitch

Circle stitch is my variation on a detached knotted chain stitch. It's a nice way to make a little circle for flowers or bubbles!

Bring the needle up at point 1. In one stitch, go down at point 2 and up at point 3, leaving the needle in place. Loosely wrap the thread over the point of the needle two times, forming a circle. Slowly pull the needle through, keeping the circle intact. Go down at point 4, then come up at point 2 and down at point 1, tacking the circle in place.

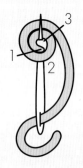
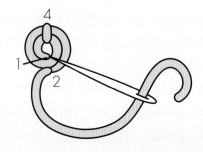

Cross Stitch

To make a cross-stitch, bring the needle up at point 1 and down at point 2. Come up at point 3 and down at point 4, completing the X.

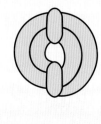
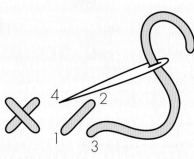

Detached Chain Stitch

Detached chain stitch is similar to the classic forward chain stitch. The only difference is that you only make one "link" at a time. There are two variations that I like to use: lazy daisy (perfect for flower petals) and scallop (perfect for critter mouths).

To make a **lazy daisy stitch**, bring the needle up at point 1 and down at point 1, leaving a small loop. Come up through the loop at point 2, then go down at point 3 (close to point 2, but not in the same hole).

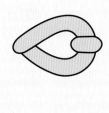
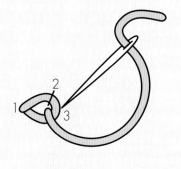

To make a **scallop stitch**, bring the needle up at point 1 and down at point 2, leaving the thread loose on the fabric surface. Come up at point 3, catching the loop of thread. Pull the thread until a scallop is formed, but not so tight that it becomes a point. Go down at point 4 (close to point 3, but not in the same hole).

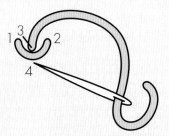

FILL STITCHES

Fill stitches are used to fill in an area, and they're a fun way to get creative with your stitching. People often think of fill stitches as making an area solid, but you can fill with any stitch and any density you want. Try scattered straight stitches, knots or cross stitches, rows of chain stitch, or the classic fill, satin stitch.

Knot Stitches

Knot stitches are an essential thing to learn, especially when stitching eyes on critters! The eyes are important for giving faces character, so be prepared to pull out a few knot stitches before you get them just right. Once the knot is formed, they are practically impossible to undo. Because of that, I like to make them with a fresh piece of floss, so that if they need to be cut out, the rest of the stitching isn't disturbed. Try out both types of knot stitches, then choose the one that works best for you.

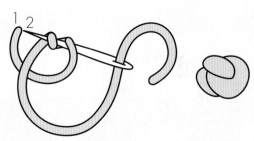

To make a **french knot**, bring the needle up at point 1. Hold the needle near the fabric and above the working thread, then wrap the thread around the needle two times. While holding the working thread, take the needle down at point 2 (close to point 1, but not the same hole). Slowly pull the needle through, holding the working thread taut until the knot is formed.

To make a **colonial knot**, bring the needle up at point 1. Form a backward C with the thread and place your needle over the C. Wrap the thread over and under the point of the needle. Then, while holding the working thread, take the needle down at point 2 (close to point 1, but not the same hole). Slowly pull the needle through, holding the working thread taut until the knot is formed.

Running Stitch

Running stitch creates a dashed line, which is great for adding darling details. You can evenly space the stitches and spaces or vary them to change up the look!

Bring the needle up at point 1 and down at point 2. Come up at point 3 and down at point 4. Repeat this process, working along your line.

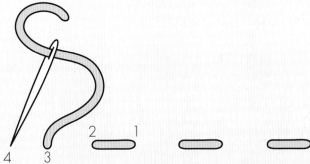

Satin Stitch

Satin stitch creates a smooth, solid area, and I especially like it for stitching noses on little animals!
Be cautious with the length of your stitches if your embroidery is on something that may get snagged.

Bring the needle up at point 1 and go down at point 2. Come up at point 3 and go down at point 4.
Repeat this process, filling in the area.

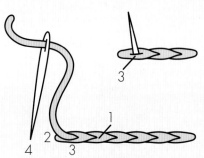

Split Stitch

Split stitch is great for bold outlines and is well named because each stitch splits the stitch before. I find that it works best with regular embroidery floss and an even number of strands.

Bring the needle up at point 1 and go down at point 2, then come up at point 3, splitting the first stitch. Go back down at point 4. Repeat this process, splitting the previous stitch as you go.

Stem Stitch

Stem stitch, despite its name, isn't used only for stems! This stitch can take a little practice, but once you've got it, you can make pretty lines of stitches that look like twisted thread lying on the fabric.

Working from left to right (reverse for left-handed stitching), bring the needle up at point 1 and down at point 2. Before pulling the stitch close to the fabric, come up at point 3, keeping the loose stitch below the needle while pulling the stitch taut. Repeat this process.

Straight Stitch

Straight stitch is about as simple and easy as stitches come! When used in a grouping to fill an area, it's sometimes called seed stitch, and it's great for adding fur texture to the animal you're stitching.

Bring the needle up at point one and down at point 2. Come up at point 3 and down at point 4, repeating for each straight stitch.

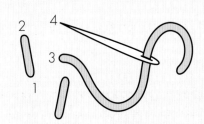

If you're going to stitch some critters, you'll need to know some basics of hand- and machine-sewing. The projects in this book use simple techniques that anyone can quickly learn. If you're already an experienced sewist, feel free to use your favorite techniques!

Sewing Kit

Sewing some crafty critters requires a few helpful tools. Although not all of the Sewing Kit items are needed for every project, you'll be glad to have them as you work your way through these projects.

SEWING KIT

Scissors
Needles
Thread
Pins
Sewing machine
Iron

Scissors:

Having a pair of good fabric scissors will make you happy when it comes to cutting your fabric. Trust me. You might also want a pair of pinking or scallop shears. They help prevent fabric from fraying and make the edge cute, too!

Needles:

As with embroidery, you'll need a needle for hand-sewing. Sharps are an all-purpose needle and a good choice to have on hand. And although they're designed with differences, your embroidery needle will also do just fine!

Thread:

I've used all-purpose thread when sewing most of the projects in this book. For hand-sewing, I usually choose hand-quilting thread because it's strong and tangles less. Choose a thread color to match your fabrics whenever possible.

Pins:

Quilters' pins, with their large, visible heads, are very useful. Not only do they hold your fabric layers together while sewing, but they are helpful for marking things and keeping cut pieces from getting lost.

Sewing Machine:

As much as I love hand-sewing, a sewing machine definitely speeds up the process! Even the most basic sewing machine will work because only straight stitching is used in these projects.

Iron:

Ironing your fabric before you start cutting and sewing makes a big difference. You'll also want an iron handy for pressing seams and for projects using fusible interfacing.

A FEW WORDS ON FABRIC

You can use just about any fabric for embroidery and sewing, but some are easier than others. My favorites are quilting cotton, linen, and wool felt. Fabrics are suggested with each project, but you can also experiment to find materials you like! If the item you're making is something that may need to be washed, it's a good idea to prewash all of your fabric before you start stitching.

Special Techniques

None of the projects in this book require advanced sewing knowledge, but being familiar with a few special techniques will help make your finished work extra special. You'll hear people exclaim, "You made this?!?"

Pressing Seams

When pressing seams, hold the iron on the seam (without scorching!), but don't slide the iron around or you may distort the sewing. The project instructions will tell you whether to press the seams open or to one side.

Clipping Curves

When you're sewing something that has curves and will be turned from wrong side to right side out, it's a good idea to clip the curves so the seam remains smooth when it gets turned. To do this, after you've sewn a seam, cut a few wedges into the seam allowance. They should look like little slices of pie, and the point should cut close to the sewing but not so close that you accidentally snip the stitches!

Appliqué

Appliqué is the process of applying a layer (or layers) of fabric onto the surface of another piece of fabric. It's perfect for creating felt faces or entire animal designs, and you can use the same technique to attach a finished piece of embroidery onto another item. Appliqué is sewn in place with stitches around the very outside edge of the top layer that you're adding. Larger pieces may need a bit of extra attachment, so fusible interfacing is helpful. Typical stitches for appliqué include blanket stitch and running stitch (all on page 115-116).

Basting

Basting is a way of holding pieces in place while you sew everything together and is a bit like pinning with thread. You can baste by hand with running stitch or on a sewing machine with long stitches.

Using Templates

For any project that has templates, you'll need to make a paper copy to work from. You can use tracing paper to trace the templates by hand, copy the template page on a photocopier, or download and print the templates from www.larkcrafts.com/bonus/?b=210. Cut the template pieces from the paper, then use them to cut out the fabric according to the project instructions. When enlarging the templates to full size, make a copy at 100%, then trim away extra items on the page. Place the templates on the copier and copy them at the percentage shown on the templates.

You can also adjust the size of the patterns to customize your project. Just be sure to enlarge or reduce all of the template pieces by the same amount.

Sewing Stitches

Hand-sewing is necessary for closing openings in plush toys and other items, as well as for some finishing work, but many projects in this book are sewn entirely by hand. Projects that rely on hand-sewing usually take a bit more patience than those made with a sewing machine, even when they are small. However, if you slow down and enjoy the process, I think you'll find that you love it!

Appliqué Stitch

Appliqué stitch is tiny and barely seen, so it's useful for when you want your appliqué stitching to be hidden. This version is great when working with felt.

Come up at point 1, between the layers. Go down through both layers at point 2, right along the edge of the top layer. Come up between the layers at point 3 and down at point 4. Repeat this process for each stitch.

Blanket Stitch

Blanket stitch works well for appliqué and creating a seam or hem with a decorative edge.

Bring the needle up at point 1, then go down at point 2 (or around the edge of the fabric) and back up at point 1. Slip the needle under the stitch to anchor it, and you're ready to start your blanket stitch. Go down at point 3 and back up at point 4, keeping the working thread under the needle. Repeat this process. To end your stitching, go under the edge of the fabric and come up at point 5 and down at point 3. Secure the thread with a knot.

Ladder Stitch

Ladder stitch is my favorite way to close up an opening. It's very secure and nearly invisible!

Hold the folded edges of the opening together. Working at the folded edge and only stitching through one layer of fabric at a time, bring the needle out at point 1. Go in at point 2, directly across from point 1. Come out at point 3 and go in at point 4, directly across from point 3. After taking a few stitches, pull the stitches taut, and continue this process.

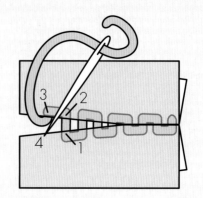

Running Stitch

Running stitch is the stitch I use most often when hand-sewing. It works for sewing a seam, quilting through several layers, appliqué, topstitching, or basting pieces in place. To create a stronger seam, sew a line of running stitch, then go back and sew another line of running stitch, this time filling in the gaps of the first, a method called holbein stitch.

For hand-sewing, running stitch works the same as with embroidery. Bring the needle up at point 1 and down at point 2. Come up at point 3 and down at point 4. Repeat this process, working along your line.

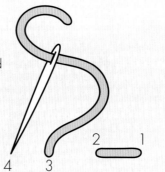

Whipstitch

Whipstitch is useful for sewing a seam and is sewn by stitching around the edge of the fabric.

Hold the layers of fabric with the edges together, either with right sides or wrong sides facing. Bring the needle through both layers, then go in at point 1 and out at point 2, stitching at an angle. Go in at point 3 and out at point 4. Repeat this process to sew the seam.

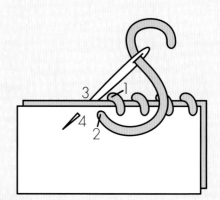

Awesome Outback Plush Trio

Visit http://larkcrafts.com/bonus/?b=210
to download project templates at full size

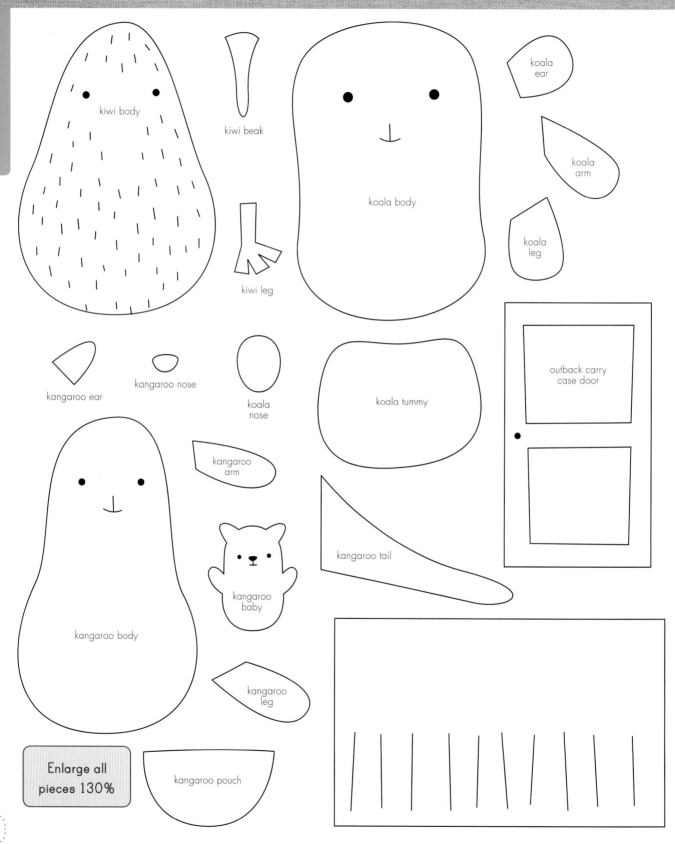

kiwi body

kiwi beak

koala
ear

koala
arm

koala body

koala
leg

kiwi leg

kangaroo ear

kangaroo nose

koala
nose

koala tummy

outback carry
case door

kangaroo
arm

kangaroo
baby

kangaroo tail

kangaroo body

kangaroo
leg

Enlarge all
pieces 130%

kangaroo pouch

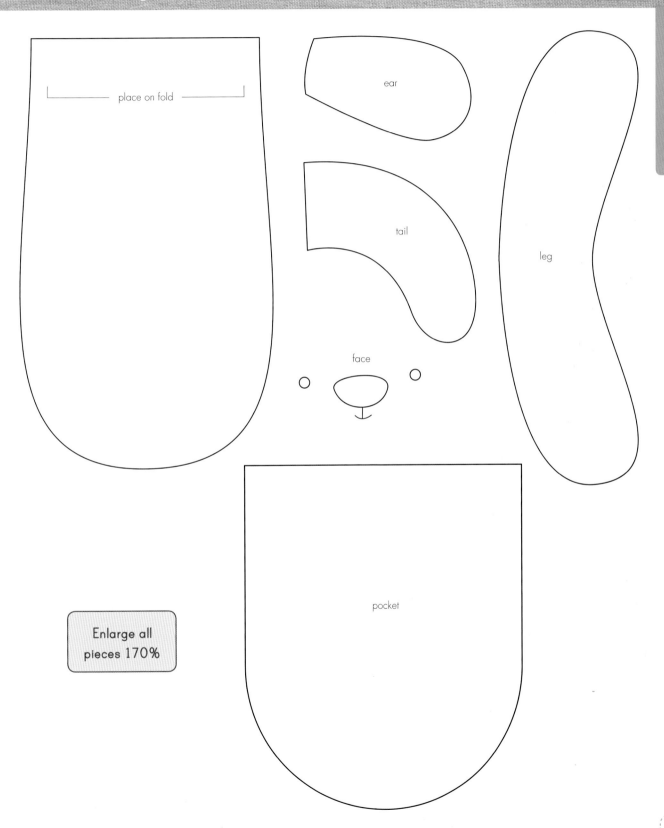

place on fold

ear

tail

leg

face

Enlarge all
pieces 170%

pocket

chipmunk body

chipmunk ears

chipmunk hat pompom

chipmunk hat

chipmunk hat trim

chipmunk backing

chipmunk hands

chipmunk tail

chipmunk feet

chipmunk wreath

chipmunk wreath bow

raccoon ears

raccoon mask

raccoon scarf knot

raccoon backing

raccoon hands

raccoon body

raccoon tail

raccoon feet

raccoon gift

Enlarge all pieces 155%

bird earmuff headband

bird earmuff (cut 2)

bird body

bird backing

bird tummy

bird lightbulb

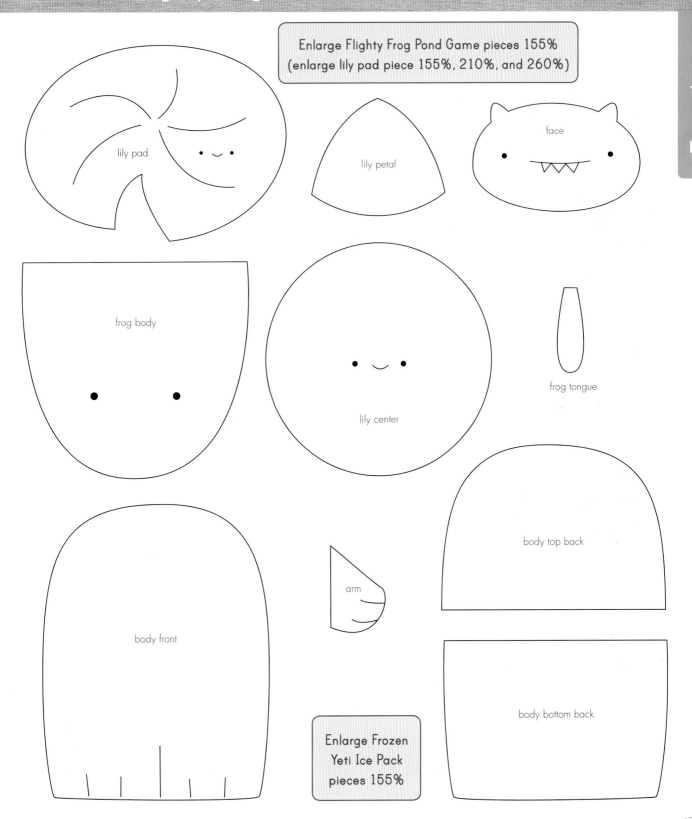

Enlarge Flighty Frog Pond Game pieces 155%
(enlarge lily pad piece 155%, 210%, and 260%)

lily pad

lily petal

face

frog body

lily center

frog tongue

body top back

body front

arm

body bottom back

Enlarge Frozen
Yeti Ice Pack
pieces 155%

Templates

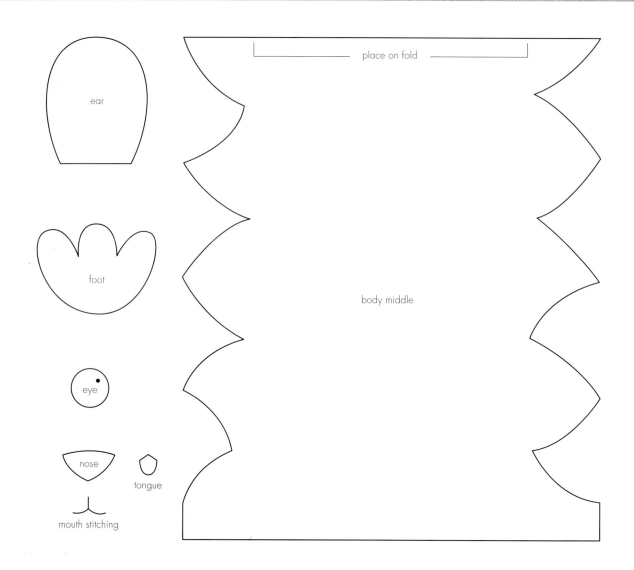

ear

foot

eye

nose

tongue

mouth stitching

place on fold

body middle

Enlarge Gleeful Guinea Pig
Plush pieces 135%.

Glowing Fireflies Jar
pieces should be used
at same size as shown.

body

wings

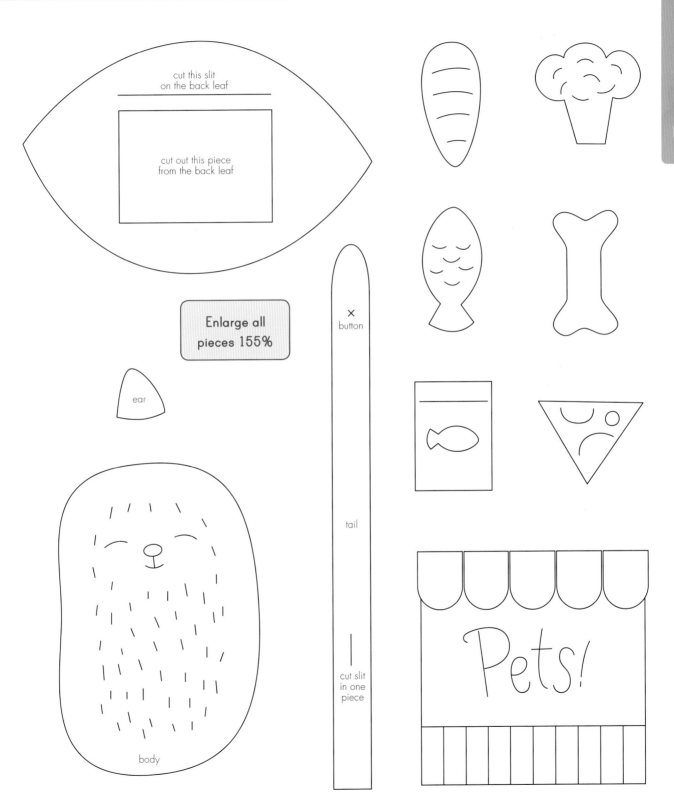

cut this slit
on the back leaf

cut out this piece
from the back leaf

Enlarge all
pieces 155%

ear

× button

tail

cut slit
in one
piece

body

Pets!

Templates

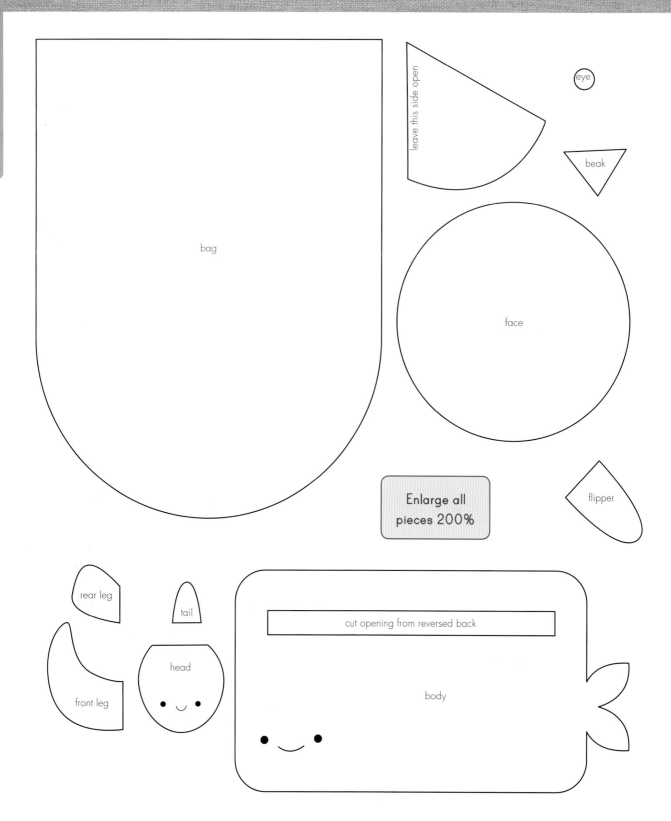

leave this side open

eye

beak

bag

face

flipper

Enlarge all
pieces 200%

rear leg

tail

front leg

head

cut opening from reversed back

body

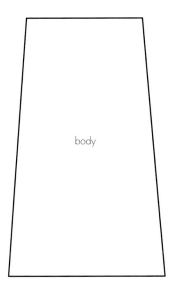

body

elephant ear
(cut 2)

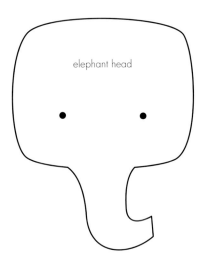

elephant head

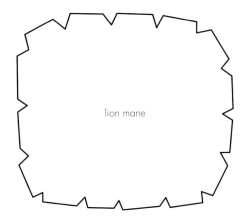

lion mane

lion head

All pieces should be used
at same size as shown.

tiger head

tiger stripe
(cut 2)

orangutan head

orangutan muzzle

giraffe head

giraffe spot
(cut 2)

giraffe horn
(cut 2)

All pieces should be used
at same size as shown.

Index

About the Author

Mollie Johanson has loved cute things, creative messes, and cuddly critters for as long as she can remember. Her blog Wild Olive is known for embroidery patterns, simply stitched projects, and playful printables, most often featuring charming creations with smiling faces. Her work has been published in *Mollie Makes*, *Australian Homespun*, and a variety of books, including several Lark Crafts titles. Mollie lives near Chicago and is happiest with a cup of coffee, some stitching, and her family close at hand.

Acknowledgments

Above all, thanks be to God, who created the critters that inspired this book and who dreamed a dream for me. Thank you to my mom for her sewing guidance and assistance, and to my family for patiently enduring my creative messes! This book would not have come to be if it weren't for Kathy Sheldon, as well as the lovely people who support my blog. Thank you to Carrie Hoge for the stunning photos, to the design team at Lark for each perfect detail, and to Brita Vallens for bringing it to completion. I'm especially appreciative of Amanda Carestio for catching the vision I had for this book and putting together the team to make it happen. Thank you!

Resources

Supplies
Whenever possible I like to buy supplies locally, but for when you need something special here are a few of my favorite sources:

www.dmc.com
www.etsy.com
www.joann.com
www.missouristarquilts.com

Resources
For the times I get stuck or need a little extra inspiration, these are some of the sites that I go to for help:

www.feelingstitchy.com
www.littledeartracks.blogspot.com
www.nanacompany.typepad.com
www.needlenthread.com
www.prettybyhand.com
www.shinyhappyworld.com
www.sublimestitching.com

31901056201421